7

The Official Tribute to

Henrik Larsson

by Joe Sullivan

© 2003

Published by Celtic FC Limited

g Designed and printed by Grange Communications Ltd, Edinburgh

ISBN: 1-902704-70-3

Contents

Introduction

1. The Double Dutch Influence   5

2. Heroes For Hire   28

3. Speaking in Tongues   52

4. The Return of the Magnificent Seven   71

5. It Was Twenty years Ago Today   115

6. Final Score Of The Swedish Rhapsody   134

7. And So The End Is Near   156

Introduction

The
Magnificent 7
needs no introduction

Chapter I
The Double Dutch Influence
Year 27BH (Before Henrik)

ON May 6, 1970 at the Giuseppe Meazza stadium, more commonly known as the San Siro, in Milan, Celtic contested their second European Cup final in three years. Still basking in the warm glory of the 1967 2-1 win over Inter Milan in Lisbon, Celtic were hot favourites to lift the trophy for the second time and, after all, few could, or would, argue with the assumption of the bookmakers and pundits.

For, after their adventures in Portugal a few summers earlier when they loosened the vice-like grip the Latin associations had on European football's top club trophy, the Celts were also the peoples' favourites. Three years earlier the well-oiled but rigidly mechanical Inter Milan were the odds-on, sure-fire favourites and few outside the proximity of Glasgow's East End gave Celtic a snowball's chance in hell of coming away from Lisbon with anything other than runners'-up medals. The unyielding and stout Catenaccio cable forged from Italian steel by Inter's manager, Helenio Herrera, was still holding strong but against all expectations Celtic stretched it to the limit, the Bhoys buckled it so much they ultimately ruptured the defensive ramparts, the chain was shattered and the drawbridge plummeted to the ground with a reverberating thud to let the football flow free.

During those 90 minutes of football under the Lisbon sun on May 25, 1967 the Internazionale Catenaccio was split asunder from one single distinct and seemingly indestructible element into 11 unconnected, redundant and broken rusted links. Celtic became the first non-Latin team to lift the continent's premier trophy and they bucked the trend with panache, bravado and more than a hint of nonchalance. They were the upstarts thumbing their noses at the hierarchy, the kids who laughed at the Emperor's new clothes; they were the Cavaliers who conquered Catenaccio. And on the Friday morning of May 26 across the length and breadth of the entire continent the punter, the man on the street, felt better for it as a new breed was beginning to stir in football. A new wave was rippling downstream from the backwater of Northern Europe - and it was lapping at the toes of the Latin masters. Football in all its pomp and glory was part of the entertainment industry once more and Celtic had helped put it there. They wore the green and white cap of European Champions with pride but there were feathers to be plucked from said cap and other teams from the frozen north took a leaf from the Celtic book. The following year, Manchester United lifted the trophy by overcoming Portugal's Benfica 4-1 at Wembley and once more the Nordic tribes had clutched the European Cup from the grasp of previous winners.

There was, however, a glitch in season 1968/69 when AC Milan, 1-0 on aggregate quarter-finalist victors over Celtic, regained the continent's top prize in Real Madrid's Bernabeu against another northern side. There was a difference this time, though, as the northern opposition didn't come from this side of the English Channel, nor were they from the burgeoning football powerhouse that Germany was fast becoming - they were from the unfancied and unfashionable football basement of The Netherlands.

On May 28, 1969 only 31,000 souls saw fit to attend the final in the vast empty expanses of the awe-inspiring Bernabeu for the AC Milan v Ajax Amsterdam conclusion in neutral Spain. The Italian side won 4-1 that night but warming the Ajax bench, as an unused substitute, was a young player barely out of his teens named Johan Cruyff. The sparse crowd may have appeared as nothing more than an unsightly and embarrassing blemish in the gargantuan canyon of the Bernabeu, but in a few years' time stadia throughout Spain would be bursting at the seams with supporters eager to catch a glimpse of the Cruyff mastery. The Spaniards were to witness an exquisite artistry and blessed skill of the beautiful game, which elevated the Dutchman to the highest pedestal. He was the only natural contender for the accolade of being the pretender to the great Pele's throne. That was still to come though. It would be 1973 before Cruyff followed his former Ajax boss Rinus Michels to Barcelona for a then massive fee of £922,300. Dutch football was still in a pupal state of metamorphosis - they had not quite attained the on-field totalitarianism within the sport that would catapult their brand of the peoples' game over the dykes of Holland and on to the centre stage of world football. Ironically, some three decades before Cruyff departed for Barcelona, it was another cross-border transfer involving the San Siro, Spain and Glasgow of all places, that kick-started Holland's rise to greatness.

Servaas 'Faas' Wilkes, who was born in 1923 in Rotterdam and started playing with youth side HION is generally regarded as the first great name in Dutch football and in the 1950s he was the No.1 hero of schoolboy Johan Cruyff, but both Faas and his brother Leen had a long history of run-ins with the Royal Dutch Football Association. The Dutch football authorities were fiercely ensconced in the amateur ethos and any form of professionalism, however tenuous the connection, was severely dealt with so when the Wilkes brothers moved from Xerxes to MVV of Maastricht for a payment of two Bedford trucks, they were suspended for one year. The two trucks were perfect for the Wilkes' 'other real job', working with 'Fa Wilkes and Zoonen', their uncle's business as a removal contractor and the brothers planned to take over the franchise. When the Dutch FA rubberstamped the suspension, the Wilkes' simply bought the trucks and moved back to play for Xerxes but the die had been well and truly cast.

The dear green place of Glasgow came into the equation on May 10, 1947 when a crowd of 130,000 turned up at Hampden Park for a showcase Great Britain v Rest of Europe clash to celebrate the re-admission of the home countries of Scotland, England and Wales to FIFA. Faas was selected for the European side and it was there in the dressing room of Hampden's old South Stand that he donned a deerstalker for a slice of Sherlock Holmes detective work and enquired as to the earnings of the Italian, French and English-based players. The continentals, represented by the cream of 10 nations and captained by Manchester United's Republic of Ireland internationalist Johnny Carey, lost 6-1 but Faas wasn't dwelling too much on the score, he had been gripped by the wanderlust and dollar signs flashed before his eyes. He had just played before 130,000 paying customers who had parted with hard-earned cash and it's little wonder that the amateur status of football in The Netherlands was even more unappealing to him then than it ever was.

Faas wasn't the first Dutch player to move abroad, that distinction fell to Bep Bakhuys, but he was certainly the most prominent and amid a search for an English club in 1948 involving a short but non-appearance flirtation with Charlton Athletic, the outcry from the Dutch football authorities was so damning that he returned to his homeland. His prodigality, in the eyes of the Dutch supremos, got the better of him though and he was soon off to Italy to join AC Milan in 1949 after being approached by a club scout, but that was the cue for some cloak and dagger skulduggery from AC's great rivals Internazionale. A few of Inter's board members, along with a local Dutch restaurant owner who acted as translator, met up with Faas and came in with an offer of more money and he quickly signed for them.

The eventual destination mattered little to the Royal Dutch Football Association who acted swiftly and Faas was suspended from international football for six years. The suspension wouldn't have held much sway with Faas, who had gone from earning six guilders a week in furniture removal to raking in 60,000 guilders a year PLUS regular salary PLUS bonuses. This was a truly massive transfer in its day and all the more so because Faas had gone from amateur status straight into the ranks of the big earners in one fell swoop. Needless to say this caused more than a few ripples of discontent within the football people of Holland. His spell with Internazionale lasted three years before a move to Torino but a serious knee operation curtailed his appearances and after one year he moved on to Spain and Valencia.

In 1955 he left Valencia to return to Holland and VVV in Venlo, partly for health reasons but there had been significant changes in the Dutch outlook to professionalism and Faas was at last able to earn money playing football in his homeland and VVV could offer him 50,000 guilders a year. The idea of paying wages to players was still frowned upon, though, and Faas still thought the Dutch FA were not yet professional enough in their outlook. He bought out his contract with VVV for 25,000 guilders in 1957 to move to Spain - once more with Valencia-based Levante as player/coach - and in their desire to attract a player of his skill, the Spanish authorities proved to be far more flexible than the Dutch.

Levante were a second division side and the Spanish league rules dictated that foreign players couldn't sign at that lower-division level. However, such was Faas' reputation, he received a one-year dispensation and was allowed to play for Levante in the hope that they would be promoted to the Primera Liga which didn't employ the no-foreigner ruling and he could then remain with the club. This was introduced under exceptional circumstances and was an indication of the towering esteem in which Faas was held. Levante failed to win the Spanish second division championship though. Winning a title was something Faas would never achieve in his 33 years of playing top-level football - amateur or otherwise, and he was on his way back to Holland.

It was a vastly different Holland he returned to though, the Royal Dutch Football Association in their wisdom had finally had enough after their most skilful player's latest migration and decided that was that. Sick of losing Faas and fearful of a mass exodus of other Dutch talent, they at last saw the light of day and by 1956 through to1957 football in Holland was fully professional at the top level. Faas played three seasons for Fortuna Sittard before, at the age of 38-years-old, returning to Xerxes, the club where it had all started for him as a 17-year-old on April 14, 1941, in a 6-1 victory over CVV. He retired from the game in season 1963/64 but despite his six-year ban from international football between 1949 and 1955 due to his Italian and Spanish sojourn, he still held an outstanding goalscoring record for the Oranje. His 35 goals in 38 international games, which would have been far more substantial but for the six-year exile, remained a Dutch best until Dennis Bergkamp broke Faas' long-standing scoring record. Bergkamp surpassed Wilkes' exploits by netting a last-minute winner in Holland's 2-1 victory over Argentina in the France '98 World Cup quarter-finals - it took Bergkamp 79 international games to beat the milestone. And even more recently, in December 2002, Patrick Kluivert, who ironically netted the opener in that Argentina game, also surpassed the 35-goal mark when he scored in a friendly against Germany - it took Kluivert 64 international games to overtake Faas.

It would be no easy task to summarise the best of the World Cup's greatest and most magical moments without making mention of giants of Dutch football like Cruyff, Bergkamp, Kluivert and many others but then again it would be difficult to imagine Holland making any imprint at all on the globe's greatest sporting tournament without the intervention of Faas Wilkes. He was the linchpin in Dutch football seeing the error of their ways and he was the crucial catalyst in their footballing authorities paving the way for Holland introduce a professional procedure, a technique and an organisation that would give birth to what would become 'Total Football.' More to the point, what hope of a Dutch team reaching a European Cup final without the steadfast resolve of this one-man protest group who, after a career of playing with "the ball seemingly attached to his feet with an invisible string", now pulled the strings when it was all but too late for him to take advantage of the situation? Many others were to benefit though, and not just those within Holland, and once professionalism had been embraced, the Dutch embarked on a not-so-long road to joining the elite of the European footballing establishment - before the end of the next decade they would be playing in the European Cup final on a level footing with one of the clubs that had previously tempted Faas away from his homeland.

The Dutch, due to their proximity to Britain, were among the first countries to have an organised Football Association. On mainland Europe only Denmark has an older FA, but the Dutch were fast learners and in 1970 after so many decades of relative inactivity it was payback time. Feyenoord had reached the European Cup final in the first ever such game between two northern sides - for the first time ever there was no Latin club in the final but the smart money was on the trophy returning to Celtic Park for the second time in three years.

That 1967 new wave ripple which tickled the toes of the Mediterranean triumvirate had swollen to a tidal upsurge, marking a sea change in European supremacy and a continental shift on the football field. There was just one slight difference for Celtic though. They were the favourites now and in those three short years since Lisbon, the Parkhead club had gone from cap-doffing peasantry to the upper echelons of European footballing aristocracy. Being the odds-on certainties, whether peoples' favourites or not, meant they had a cross to bear. They were the elite, the establishment and they were now the hierarchy they had battled so valiantly to topple just three summers earlier. The dialectic theory had kicked in quickly in big-style and the team from Rotterdam were the new insolent kids on the block champing at the bit to don the rags of David and slay the Glaswegian Goliaths. The rigidity and sheer weight of that cross breaking Celtic's back wasn't helped in any manner by the hefty nails they had well and truly sledge-hammered in during the semi-finals of the previous month.

Celtic faced the might of Don Revie's Leeds United, so cross-border rivalry ensured the pairing was rightly given the billing of 'Clash of the Century' and even with the aid of 20/20 hindsight, it's difficult to argue with the early spin-doctors who christened the two-legged tie thus. The three hours of football has imprinted its own chapter in the Celtic history books but may also have engraved the epitaph on the tombstone of the club's European Cup ambitions that season. Returning to Glasgow with a 1-0 first leg win at Elland Road, the stage was set for a night of glory at Hampden when Celtic completed the job to win 2-1 on the night in front of 136,505 supporters crammed into the crater that was Europe's largest football arena. But the virtue of 20/20 hindsight also conjures up images of Celtic winning the 'final before the final' and if the press, punters, pundits, and the bookies were to believed, the Bhoys just had to turn up in Milan, lift up the European Cup and leave on the next available flight back to Glasgow.

Feyenoord had other ideas, however, and such was Faas Wilkes' impact in his three years with Internazionale that a framed picture of him still hangs in the San Siro. With that in mind, it's not too difficult to visualise the Feyenoord players as they arrived at the stadium giving more than a cursory glance at the framed still of Wilkes who, in those Dutch pre-glory days, was the greatest native exponent of their trade and a hero to each and every one of them all in their boyhoods. They may or may not have given thought to the concept that if it hadn't been for Faas they may not have been there in Milan but history meant nothing that night - for both sides it would seem.

It was a night the Bhoys would rather forget. If the semi-final against Leeds United forged its own episode in the Celtic annals, then the final itself merits little more than a footnote at the bottom of the chapter's last page. Celtic lost 2-1 after extra-time on a lacklustre night, when even the renowned vocal and vociferous Celtic supporters suffered the effects of culture shock as the massed klaxons and horns of the Dutch fans created a wall of sound which, and not for the last time, reverberated around Europe. For all we know, Inter aficionados may look back on Lisbon 1967 as Celtic supporters view Milan 1970. It just wasn't our night, but would lifting Europe's most cherished club prize elevate Feyenoord to the status of hierarchy in the same manner that the accolade had help ensure Celtic's rise to prominence - or would it be a one-off with the Rotterdam side being nothing more than a flash in the pan? After all, the grounds for such a hypothesis were there for all to see. Hadn't Celtic become victims of believing the hyperbole in winning the 'final before the final'.

Wasn't there rumour of the players spending more time talking bonuses than talking tactics? Weren't there allegations of the players lazing around in the blazing Italian sun when three years previously they were shielded from not only the heat but everything else? And, more to the point, couldn't this just have been one of those nights? After all, on a bad night any team from anywhere could have beaten

Celtic at any stage of any competition - it does happen and European Cup finals, the crème de la crème, are not immune to such an eventuality.

All such allegations and conjecture mattered not a jot to Feyenoord, however, who were in the throes of ecstasy in celebrating the greatest night so far in Dutch football history. They had triumphed where a year before their arch rivals Ajax had failed. But the questions still had to be asked - were Feyenoord masquerading as European champions at the expense of more worthy adversaries and could Dutch football maintain its surprising run of appearing in two consecutive European Cup finals? The poser would soon be answered as the winning tide was beginning to ebb away from Glasgow and anywhere else in Europe you care to mention and flow towards Holland, but unfortunately for Feyenoord, it meandered to the skeletal canals of Amsterdam rather than arriving at Rotterdam. Ajax, inspired by the indomitable Cruyff, embarked on an astounding sequence of victorious European Cup finals, a winning progression not seen since the amazing domination of the magnificent Real Madrid side of the late 1950s, when they held a monopoly on the competition by winning the first five tournaments in a row.

Holland was now controlling the European Cup cartel, with Ajax winning the next three consecutive finals, triumphing first 2-0 over Panathinaikos at Wembley in 1971 before beating Inter Milan by the same scoreline in Rotterdam of all places, then finally defeating Juventus 1-0 in 1973's conclusion in Belgrade. Indeed, it has to be said, mainly due to the subsequent intervention of the English and the Germans, no Latin side would win the European Cup between AC Milan's 1969 victory over Ajax and the 1985 Juventus win over Liverpool in the ill-fated Heysel Stadium final in Brussels. Celtic's further involvement in a European final was cast to the wind, a cold and depressing gale that would eerily whistle and squall around Paradise for some 33 years, but a character who was to play an early part in abating, though not completely buffeting, that chilling gust was on duty on that night of May 6, 1970 in the San Siro.

The legendary Jock Stein was, of course, Celtic manager at both of their European Cup finals and although he would be only the fourth incumbent of the Parkhead hot seat in the first 90 years of the club's existence, fate decreed that several other Celtic managers would have had more than a vested interest in the outcome that night in Milan - especially the three on the pitch. Stein was there obviously, former manager Jimmy McGrory would have witnessed the action, as would future manager Lou Macari, who was then part of the Celtic squad. A 13-year-old Tommy Burns, who signed an S-form for Celtic that year, would have been an enthralled viewer as, no doubt were other future managers in the shape of Liam Brady, Jozef Venglos and Martin O'Neill. But of the three on the park it was the least likely of the trio who was to first lay the foundations that would help bring a wind of change to Celtic's European final hopes ... Enter one Willem Jansen.

However, if you had asked any Celtic supporter on May 6, 1970 to make a list of possible candidates for the job of Celtic manager in the future from the 24 players who played that night, the best placing 23-year-old Jansen could possibly have hoped for would 13th - behind the 12 Celtic players who played in Milan. It wasn't just that Celtic fans would have had trouble pronouncing never mind recognising the names of the Feyenoord players, it's simply that Celtic were a Scottish team and Scottish teams just did not import managers. More to the point, Celtic always employed former players as managers and, of course, from the team that night, Bhoys' legends Billy McNeill (twice) and Davie Hay were to go on and manage the club. However, although Cruyff was to be the darling of the Dutch fans, not to mention the most instantly recognisable player in European football, and Ajax were to overshadow Feyenoord on the continental stage, Wim Jansen was not to be totally eclipsed while the Rotterdam side were put in the shade by their arch rivals. Far from it, he and Cruyff were embarking on a close friendship that lasts to this day and while the Ajax maestro, along with national team-mates Johan Neeskens, Ruud Krol, Arie Haan, Johnny Rep and Gerry Muhren were to form the backbone of the Holland side that would draw gasps of delight from football fans throughout the world.

The likes of Jansen and Feyenoord team-mates, Willem Suurbier and Willem van Hanegem, were also an integral part of the Oranje team that presented Total Football to the biggest stage - the World Cup finals. It goes without saying that the rise of the Oranje on the world stage could not have happened without the burgeoning development of club football in Holland and that the professionalism inspired by Faas Wilkes played a vital part in their emergence as a world power.

True to form for the Royal Dutch Football Association, their amateur stance, due to having basically every single Dutch player apart from supposed renegades like Wilkes to choose from, probably presented them with reasonable success on the dwindling amateur world circuit but played havoc with Holland's chances against the big boys. They had Olympic medals to show, with bronze gongs for four competitions in a row between 1905 and 1924, but little else. They understandably faired worse in competition against true professionals and considering their rise to prominence in the 1970s; they were also-rans on the international stage. They didn't enter the first World Cup in 1930, in 1934 and 1938 they didn't progress past the first game, they did not enter in 1950 or 1954 and failed to qualify for 1958, 1962, 1966 or 1970.

That was to change, though, and quickly. The transformation mirrored that of their domestic clubs and enraptured millions when they reached 1974's final in West Germany, and on the road there they defeated Argentina (4-0) and the then current holders Brazil (2-0). They had the misfortune to meet 'home' side West Germany in the Munich final and narrowly lost 2-1. Their quest for world domination continued and in 1978 they were World Cup finalists for the second successive tournament, and this time they not only famously disposed of Scotland but out-pointed West Germany and Italy in the second group stage, only to come up once more against the 'home' side, this time in the shape of Argentina. On this occasion the final went to extra-time and although the Dutch lost 3-1, their place as world giants in football was secured.

Their elevation also ensured that Wim Jansen had played in two consecutive World Cup finals and, thanks to Archie Gemmill's wonder-goal for Scotland against the Dutch, warranted him a place in Scottish film history. Jansen was one of the Dutchmen bamboozled by Gemmill's mazy and momentous run before scoring. The goal was included in the adaptation of Irvine Welsh's groundbreaking Trainspotting novel and, therefore, Jansen was immortalised as the Celtic manager who appeared the classic 1996 film. By a quirk of fate, some of the movie's pub scenes were shot in the London Road Tavern - little more than a free-kick away from Celtic Park.

However, imprinting their authority on club football and rising from also-rans to World Cup finalists ensured that the pride of Holland were on show in the biggest shop window of them all and greedy eyes throughout Europe beheld the Dutch renovation enviously before checking out their bank accounts and booking a KLM flight to Schipol Airport. Prior to Faas Wilkes, the only Dutch masters to leave Holland were stunning works by the likes of Vincent van Gogh and Rembrandt or maybe even a pack of the famous cigars, but as the modern-day revolution gathered force and gained momentum, Johan Cruyff certainly wasn't going to be the only big-name star to pack up and head for pastures new. Many more were all to widen their horizons and spread the Dutch gospel far beyond the environs of Europe's lowlands - from the likes of Johnny Rep in 1976 through to Ruud Gullit, Marco van Basten and Frank Rijkaard. This is a state of affairs that has continued to this day, with players such as Ruud van Nistelrooy, and at first deliberation would seem to go against the grain of Dutch football's plan to keep their best players by introducing professionalism.

That, however, in modern-day Holland, isn't the case and now the laissez faire perspective adopted by The Netherlands as a people in general is reflected in the Dutch FA's pursuance of the promotion of their players and their game abroad. So much so that when Pierre van Hooijdonk joined Celtic from NAC Breda in 1994, the 'agent' was actually an equivalent of a Players' Union representative from the Dutch FA overseeing the welfare and interests of one of their members. The remarkable and indispensable Dutch youth development system has ensured that there is always a conveyor belt of talented youngsters eager to impress and with the obvious skills to step into the shoes of departing players, but no matter how fast the production line churns them out, there was no doubt that the dilution of home-grown domestic power would have an effect on the potency of the Dutch league. The answer to the problem was paradoxically simple enough. If you have a dearth of talent through export then rectify the situation through import ... Enter one Henrik Larsson.

By 1993, Wim Jansen was coach at Feyenoord and neither he nor his new 22-year-old Swedish signing from Helsinborgs IF would have given Celtic a second thought back then. Jansen may have reminisced about Milan occasionally, but appearing in two World Cup finals may have clouded some of the shine from the European Cup win, and this young Larsson chappie may have swotted up on his new club's history but he wasn't even born when Feyenoord triumphed in 1970. Phrases like the 'poisoned chalice' of Celtic managership and 'stopping the 10' would have meant absolutely nothing to Jansen, while 'The Magnificent Seven' and 'King of Kings' would have Larsson wondering what on earth a 1960 Western and a hymn had to do with football, never mind him. But the two first crossed paths in September of that year, although Larsson couldn't actually wear the colours of Feyenoord until November as part of a pre-contract deal with former club Helsinborgs, and clauses in the player's contracts were to play a major part in the striker finally arriving at Celtic in 1997.

That was still a long way off, though, and by the time a six-year-old Henrik Larsson first started knocking a ball about with local club Hogaborg BK, Wim Jansen was still playing football at the top level with Feyenoord. Born in Rotterdam on October 28, 1946, Jansen joined Feyenoord in 1966 and, 474 appearances and 41 goals later, he took the Atlantic crossing in 1980 to join the Washington Diplomats. During that time, apart from winning the European Cup against Celtic of course, he also lifted the World Club Championship, three Dutch titles and one Dutch Cup as well as playing in the 1974 UEFA Cup final 4-2 aggregate win over Tottenham Hotspur. His stateside stint didn't finish his playing career as, after just 29 appearances in America, he returned to Holland to sign up for Feyenoord's arch rivals Ajax and between 1980 and 1982 made 51 appearances for the Amsterdam club. Jansen's long and illustrious club career which was partnered by 65 Dutch international appearances (that delivered a solitary goal for the future Celtic manager) was the perfect grounding for an automatic turn to coaching on his retiral from the playing side of the game. And from 1982 to 1987 he took over the reins as Feyenoord youth team coach before the bug bit him and he took a shot at first-team management. That resulted in a move to neighbouring Belgium to coach Lokeren in season 1987/88 but he quit after just six months and took up a post back home in Holland as coach with SVV Dordrecht in 1988. He left in March 1990 when the call came again from the mighty Feyenoord.

He was appointed head coach with old team-mate Wim van Hanegem and won the Dutch Cup in 1990/91. His post then became that of technical director and they retained the cup in 1992, then reached semi-finals of Cup-Winners' Cup and clinched the league title in 1993 for the first time in nine years. He quit in December 1993 but who would imagine that a few years later he would uncannily repeat the extraordinary feat of leading a club to championship glory after a nine-year drought and then leave soon after? Jansen's next port of call was in the Middle East when he took up the role of assistant coach to Leo Beenhakker in charge of the Saudi national team in 1994. Both were sacked after four months in the job because their training methods were judged too severe. In 1995 he moved further east to the land of the rising sun to coach J-League side Hiroshima Sanfrecce but failed to repeat his earlier successes and returned to Rotterdam in 1997.

The job offers weren't slow in coming in for a coach of Jansen's calibre, though, and he was strongly linked with technical director's post at Ajax before he received a call from the other side of the North Sea. Jansen had a healthy habit of turning around the fortunes of clubs in the straits of despair and the 1990s were anything but joyous for the green and white hordes who spent every other Saturday trudging wearily along to Celtic Park wrapped in a cold overbearing sense of duty rather than in a warm glow of anticipation at reaching the end of a long dark tunnel. The nightmare '90s were a solemn sojourn from the swaggering swing of the '60s, the glitzy glam of the '70s and the vibrant new romance delivered by the centenary decade of the '80s. The only thing going faster than Celtic going through managers was Rangers going through championships and, try as they might, the Parkhead side couldn't stem the flow of title trophies heading towards Ibrox.

The first phase of the decade had already seen off managers Billy McNeill, Liam Brady, Lou Macari and Tommy Burns as Rangers turned the screw but in season 1996/97, Celtic choked on the bitterest pill of all. Arch rivals Rangers had equalled Celtic's long-standing and proud record of nine consecutive league titles and as the Ibrox side splashed the cash to bolster their armoury, it seemed that the only item missing was a heat-seeking missile to home in on number 10. Celtic needed someone at the helm to keep a calm head while all around him, mainly those around the pitch watching the action, were losing theirs and Wim Jansen fitted the bill. His tactical awareness had revolutionised many teams and he turned down up to a dozen clubs before taking up the Celtic offer and signing on the dotted line on Thursday, July 3, 1997.

The new manager said: "I had other offers from Holland to consider, but I wanted to wait for a really big club. The stadium, the support and the history of Celtic attracted me and the club always has a special place in my memories. Celtic was involved in the greatest day of my career, when I played against them in Feyenoord's European Cup winning side of 1970 and I want to take them back to the highest level. The challenge is as big as any I have faced in my career but I welcome it. I am delighted to be joining a famous club."

The appointment was a bolt from the blue and the nature of the secrecy surrounding his engagement gave birth to some not so welcoming headlines. In particular, his spell in Japan with Sanfrecce provoked the explosive and unpalatable "The second worst thing to hit Hiroshima". The negativity was not sparked purely by the tight security encircling the announcement. There was an element of anonymity about Jansen and, to be fair, the Scottish press knew little of his exploits. However, the plaudits rolled in from those in the know, those who had played with, those who worked alongside and those who been tutored by Jansen.

The great Johan Cruyff, who once stated that Jansen was one of only four men in the world worth talking to about football, said: "I have been in touch with Celtic to congratulate them on the appointment of a top class coach in Wim Jansen. It is a massive statement of Celtic's ambition and I've no doubt that he will be a big success."

Former Feyenoord winger, Gaston Taument, who was then with Benfica, said: "Wim Jansen is the best coach I've worked with. When he came to Feyenoord the club were at rock bottom and on the verge of bankruptcy. But what Wim achieved was quite incredible. When he left, Feyenoord had won the Dutch championship once and the cup twice." Chelsea's Dutch goalkeeper, Ed de Gooey, added: "Celtic could not wish for a better man. He is the only coach in Holland, apart from Cruyff, who knows how to play true attacking football." And praise came from an unlikely source when former darling of the Rangers support Pieter Huistra, who played under Jansen in Japan, said: "Wim is an outstanding coach - the best I've ever worked with. Celtic players maybe do not know too much about him, but they will very soon. He will talk them through everything he wants done and they will learn to appreciate that he knows better than them. The job is perfect for him. I know he has waited for the right offer and this is the one for him."

As luck would have it, Jansen's first field trip with his new charges was a bit of a busman's holiday for him - straight back to Holland for Celtic's pre-season tour. It was a touch reminiscent of the couple from Margate on holiday in South Wales who decided to go on a Mystery

Tour day-trip and the bus took them straight back to their home town! While the rest of the charabanc party took in the delights of the Kent seaside town, the unimpressed pair just went home for a cup of tea. Jansen was on his own Mystery Tour though and whether it turned out to be of The Beatles' magical variety or not would be down to nothing more than sheer hard work and there was no time for nipping home for a cuppa. It's doubtful, however, that the first game of the tour solved any of his queries as the Celts fired a 21-goal salute to him by thrashing FC Beatrix 21-0.

On the face of it, after the Beatrix slaughter, there was the irony that it didn't look like he needed to look for a striker but deeper down, no-one - players, supporters or, more importantly, Jansen himself was taking anything more than quiet contentment at the overwhelming scoreline. Jansen said: "I am using the Holland trip to judge the players. Good ones you can spot in a minute, the others may need longer to assess. If we need to make signings, we will bring in players who will play for the team. Even great stars like my friend Johan Cruyff knew the value of playing for the good of the side. That was what worked for me in Feyenoord and what will always work in football. Achieving success will not be about my philosophy or systems but having quality players who can make an effective contribution to the team."

Clairvoyance may not have been one the personal qualities marked down by Jansen on the CV he presented to Celtic nor, indeed, one of the criteria listed in the job descriptions demanded by managing director Fergus McCann through general manager Jock Brown. But he must have been watching the Beatrix game through a crystal ball if the final sentence of his post-match commentary is anything to go by. "Achieving success will not be about my philosophy or systems but having quality players who can make an effective contribution to the team." It may be a bit wordy for a slogan but Henrik Larsson's agent could have done a lot worse than having a few T-shirts ran off with those very words printed under the dreadlocked one's face - with the final five words italicised - effective contribution to the team - surely a slight understatement in view of what was to unfold over the coming seasons.

Not that Rob Jansen - no relation to Wim - and Larsson's agent, had much trouble in promoting his client to his namesake at Celtic Park. Wim didn't need telling of just how remarkable Larsson's talents were, all he needed to know was the state of play in the striker's relationship with his current employers and the answer was, to put it ever so mildly, appalling.

King Henry the Sixth, Part II (Act IV, Scene II)
"The first thing we do, let's kill all the lawyers."

So said Dick to the rebel Jack Cade in William Shakespeare's chronicle of a previous King Henke, but in the summer of 1997, Henrik Larsson's love affair with Feyenoord in general, and manager Arie Haan in particular had deteriorated to the extent that he may well have agreed with Dick's bloodthirsty proposal. The disillusioned striker may also have empathised with the rebel's answer that included: "I did but seal once to a thing, and I was never mine own man since."

So disenchanted had he become with the situation in Rotterdam that Larsson was all but ready to relinquish his dream of returning to Sweden as a hero and accept that he had failed by returning to play with Helsinborgs if they could come to a financial agreement with Feyenoord. There was even the possibility, however remote, that Larsson would have to turn the Faas Wilkes philosophy on its head by reverting back to amateurism on his return to his homeland and maybe even have to take a year out of the game due to Swedish FA rulings regarding returning professionals. The background to the whole murky scenario was obscured with red tape but there should have been no reason for such bureaucracy as it was as clear as day that Larsson and his agent were in the right. The reason for the complicated procedure behind Larsson's problems in getting away from Feyenoord was a clause in his contract stating that if a team came in with a certain offer - in this case the bottom limit was £600,000 - he could leave. On the face of it the agreement was watertight and legally binding but the men who ran the Rotterdam club, for whatever reason, saw things differently. It was clear that they didn't see him as an integral part of their team so, that not being the answer to their obvious reluctance to part company with the striker, the only palpable motive could be more money. The roots of the Swede's predicament went a lot deeper than that and Larsson at least hoped he was just coming to the end of a very long nightmare.

Larsson signed for Feyenoord from Helsinborgs in September 1993 for a fee of £295,000, which even back then wasn't a great deal of money, but half of that sum went to his first club Hogaborg as part of the deal which saw him move between the two Swedish clubs in 1991. He had been toying with a move to Switzerland and Grasshoppers of Zurich, as they were the first foreign club to offer some serious money for the striker. However, Larsson soon learned of Feyenoord's interest and, although the paperwork with the Swiss club was more or less finalised, after that there really wasn't much of a decision for him to make. It transpired that Feyenoord had been keeping tabs on the prolific goalgetter and they were keen to snap up his talents. It didn't take long for Larsson to weigh up his options and his dream move to one of the top clubs from one of the most well-respected and toughest leagues in Europe was on.

It was a dream that would eventually turn sour as in the first few short months he was there he had forged a relationship with Feyenoord's team director Wim Jansen, but before the year was out his aspiring mentor was on his way through the exit door. Jansen's former team-mate at Rotterdam, Willem van Hanegem, was still running affairs and Larsson became a valued member of a successful Feyenoord team. It was clearly evident why this massive Dutch club had moved for the young Swede who had an instinctive eye for goals. After moving up through the ranks at various age levels with Hogaborg, he made his debut for the senior team aged 17-years-old while they were still in the Swedish Third Division. In 64 games for the minnow club he found the net on 23 occasions and was soon catching the eye of Helsinborgs, the bigger club in the area. Prior to the move, Larsson at 18 years of age or so was taking stock of his life and in realising that football wasn't the be all and end all, he wasn't very far away from giving the game up all together - amazingly, considering what was to transpire, football wasn't everything to him. Circumstances were soon to change, though, and in three short years he had moved up the divisions one by one from third to premier on the first steps that would lead to him becoming a Swedish icon.

At 21-years-old, Larsson heard through the grapevine that Helsinborgs were sniffing around and although they were only a semi-pro team, the move would still be a step upwards for the youngster. He was still carrying out his day job duties as a fruit packer when he received a phone call from Helsinborgs stating their interest. A friend drove Larsson down to the meeting and he signed on there and then for £300 a month without any bonus payments. The second division outfit's latest acquisition fired in 34 goals that season and hoisted Helsinborgs into to the top division for the first time in 22 long years. Life was obviously tougher in the Swedish Premier League but Larsson still was among the country's top scorers that season with 16 goals and notes were being taken in the stands followed by mobile phone calls back to Rotterdam - Feyenoord were on the prowl and as soon as they heard Grasshoppers were interested they pounced to make sure they got their man. However, as so often is the instance in football - in Celtic's case a prime example is from 1926 when chief scout Steve Callaghan went to check on an outfielder in Fife but came away with the signature of a young keeper named John Thomson, Larsson wasn't on the shopping list when Jansen watched Helsinborgs as he was there to scout another player. So not for the first time, impulse buying would have a massive effect on the history of Celtic Football Club.

Thanks to Wim on a whim, the Dutch club were not only moving in on a proven goalscorer, they were investing £295,000 of their money in a player who had demonstrated that he could up the ante as he stepped another rung up the ladder. His 23 goals for Hogaborg in 64 games registered at just over one counter in every three games - his strike-rate when he moved up a level, however, was nearly a goal a game with 50 goals in just 56 matches for Helsinborgs. The Dutch side knew they were getting a winner and but for some bizarre and truly nonsensical decisions in tactics and team selection, Larsson could still be winning games for Feyenoord to this day. The arrival of Arie Haan as the new Feyenoord top dog signalled the beginning of the end for Larsson and his long nightmare period was about to darken his hopes and dreams of really making the grade at the top level.

Looking back at Larsson's strike rate during his four years in Rotterdam, 26 goals in 101 games, it would seem that the rich vein of golden goals had well and truly dried up. That would be dramatically oversimplifying the matter though. Haan, for whatever reason, simply didn't seem to take a shine to one of the most prodigious up-and-coming talents in Swedish, Dutch and European football and his positional sense as a football tactician seemed to have deserted him in the case of Larsson. Dear reader, whatever you do, if by some weird and wonderful chance the opportunity ever arises, don't let Haan practice Feng Shui in your house as the television screen would probably be facing the wall and the sofa placed against the door - in the kitchen - if his positional directions to the Swede are anything to go by. Larsson was here, there and everywhere on matchdays and 'everywhere' included the dugout bench if he was lucky enough to get a place on it as Haan took squad rotation to a new level by rotating the striker around the pitch on a game-by-game basis.

Larsson switched from left wing to right wing and back faster and more frequently than Tony Blair. He was played in midfield or anywhere Haan saw fit to play him and, to make matters worse, the new coach gave no explanation or indication as to why he was adopting that policy. It wasn't as if Larsson wasn't coming up with the answers when the right questions were asked of him on the pitch, he had won two consecutive Dutch Cup medals with Feyenoord in 1994 and 1995 and picked up a third-place World Cup medal in the USA in 1994 by scoring in the play-off against Bulgaria. Nonetheless, he rarely played a full game for Haan and was usually substituted or worse still, was listed on the bench so many times that he actually grew to hate and loathe the tracksuit he was wearing.

King Henry the Sixth, Part III (Act III, Scene III)
"Having nothing, nothing can he lose."

Another King Henke prophecy from the prescient Bard, this time uttered by the Earl of Warwick in the presence of Queen Margaret and King Louis XI of France and as Larsson weighed up the pros and cons of his rapidly diminishing job satisfaction, he resolved to take some drastic and dramatic action. Something had to give and Larsson decided that it wasn't going to be his football career or his personal home life relationship with Magdalena whom he had met when he was 19-years-old - they had been inseparable ever since. The situation was affecting his life away from football and now even the Dutch press were beginning to nitpick about his performances regardless of the fact that he was played out of position. Haan had made Larsson's life, both professional and personal, hell for fully 18 months and without the support of Magdalena it would have been unbearable, so it was hardly surprising the striker was coming to the end of his tether, his agent was told to get the feelers out for another club - any club. Larsson opened his heart to a Swedish newspaper, publicly stating his wish to leave Feyenoord and, of course, the news filtered back to Rotterdam. To put it mildly, the situation got worse for Larsson and matters were to deteriorate further before they got better thanks to a phone call from Dutch journalist, Marcel van der Kram, to Wim Jansen who had just taken over the reins at yet another new club - Celtic.

The plot thickened beyond all comprehension now as Celtic placed Larsson at the top of their shopping list but, more importantly, Larsson positioned the Glasgow giants firmly at the top of his wish list just as soon as he had answered the good news call from his agent Rob Jansen. Celtic were on the scene now and far from being delighted at the apparent opportunity to offload an unhappy player they had evidently no intention of making part of their plans, Feyenoord did all they could with more than smattering of a Machiavellian stroke to scupper the proposed move. Despite Larsson's £600,000 clause, Feyenoord wanted £1.8million for a player they seemingly didn't rate and even the most liberal use of artistic license couldn't portray the illusion that they were using the big asking price as a scare tactic to keep the player. The big worry for Celtic was that the £1.8million tag would attract another club, or clubs, and start a bidding war, an outcome that would have been right up Feyenoord's street. Other underhand actions and dastardly deeds were attempted by the Rotterdam club, with perhaps the most devious and deceitful being the alleged proposal to Larsson that if he held out for the £1.8million he could pocket £600,000 himself.

Considering Feyenoord didn't know what to do with Larsson on the pitch, their tactics off it were very imaginative indeed and the striker laughed the dirty trick campaign out of court. However, court was exactly where the whole shebang was going to end up as the player was not only determined to leave Feyenoord but was also equally resolute that he was going to wear the green and white of Celtic. Larsson still had two years of his contract with Feyenoord left to run but the £600,000 clause overrode all else and, on paper at least, left the ball firmly in the player's court. However that still had to be made crystal clear and such was Feyenoord's filibustering, a Dutch soccer tribunal decreed they would have to splice the red tape and that would take time. This was yet another heartbreaking blow for the player who was at his wit's end with all the unnecessary brouhaha connected with what seemed like a simple straight-forward move from one professional club to another.

Larsson was in Limbo and Haan simply wasn't helping matters by demonstrating a lack of diplomacy and tact that, depending on how you look at it, let the striker know exactly where he stood or would keep him in a quandary as to what lay in store for him. Larsson was singled out by being subject to the punishing toil of the typical pre-season pain sessions in the morning but expelled from training games and ball work in the afternoon. If Haan was going to be punitive then Larsson decided that two could play at that game and imposed upon himself a term of solitary confinement by refusing to train with the rest of the Feyenoord squad. Then, on July 21, just when the player thought he would never get the move he so dearly wanted, he pressed the Teletext button on the remote control and the news from the Dutch FA's tribunal at their Zeist headquarters flashed up "Tribunal says Larsson can go." Those five words were as Manna from heaven as he left purgatory and the golden road was free of Feyenoord's obstacles and clear for a move to Paradise.

Davie Hay is in no doubt that the credit for signing Larsson should go to Wim Jansen, but the former Celt was heavily involved in the transfer negotiations from day one. He recalled: "Really it was all to do with Wim when we realised that this player who had been recommended to us named Henrik Larsson was available at a price we could afford, namely £650,000. But we were intent on going through everything in fine detail as there were a couple of complications in the earlier Dutch deal that brought Pierre van Hooijdonk to Glasgow. These didn't arise until later so we wanted to make sure the contract with Henrik was satisfactory for all involved. I was actually with the team in Holland so I didn't have far to travel. We had a good relationship with Bob Maaskant, who was heavily involved in the Pierre transfer, so he and Henrik's agent, Rob Jansen, were at the meeting. This meeting in Gouda was really to break the ice and I remember at the time Henrik's and Magdalena's son Jordan had just been born but Henrik was really quiet at the meeting. He never spoke a lot and, to be honest, I don't even think he'll remember me being there.

"The whole thing was possible thanks to Rob Jansen's negotiation of the price clause in Henrik's original contract with Feyenoord, but I didn't have the authority to sanction the signing - that would have had to come from Fergus McCann, so I phoned Jock Brown with the details and we got the go ahead. After that, things went reasonably smoothly in the case of terms between the player and Celtic but then Feyenoord threw a spanner into the works and what seemed like a straightforward transfer became complicated. But we just had to bide our time and in the end we had who I truly believe to be Celtic's best ever signing. In my opinion he is up there with the best. I'm not old enough to have seen Jimmy McGrory but in my day Jimmy Johnstone and Kenny Dalglish were the two greatest players ever in my estimation and Henrik is up there with them. Jinky would just edge out Henrik as the greatest Celt I've ever seen but Henrik is definitely, without doubt, Celtic's greatest ever signing and he truly deserves all the accolades bestowed upon him."

King Henry the Sixth, Part III (Act III, Scene III)
"Henry now lives in Scotland at his ease."

Shakespeare really did miss his vocation in life as his King Henke predictions clearly illustrate, instead of regaling us all with that medieval nonsense about men in tights, he should have put his quill to better use between the horoscope and sports pages in the 16th century tabloids. Larsson jetted in to Glasgow and duly signed for Celtic on Friday, July 25, 1997 after the long, petty and ultimately futile delaying tactics by Feyenoord. At that point Larsson had won 28 caps for Sweden and scored seven goals. Ironically, he earned his most recent cap playing at Ibrox in September 1996 in the World Cup qualifying game which Scotland won 1-0. The Celts had already kicked a ball in anger for the first time that season when, two days before Larsson signed on the dotted line, they had travelled down to Wales on UEFA Cup duty and defeated Inter CableTel 3-0. Larsson's first public appearance as a Celt arrived in the following week's return leg but he took no part in the 5-0 rout of the Cardiff side. Instead, he was introduced to the 41,537-strong crowd at half time by drawing the club's matchday lottery - the Paradise Windfall. Few, including a delighted Thomas Cairns from Coatbridge who pocketed the £3,000 prize that night, would have guessed then that the dreadlocked Swede would prove to be the biggest Paradise Windfall ever, with goals raining in from all angles and

Celtic had bought the winning ticket for the knock-down price of £650,000.

The spanking brand new Celt was delighted that his nightmare was over and proverbially over the moon that not only had he joined the club he had set his sights on but also that he was again linking up with a coach who rated him and knew exactly where to position him on the pitch. There was also the added bonus that his new contract with his new club had no strings attached and everything was above board with a definite air of gentlemen's agreements about the whole affair. He said: "I won't be expecting a pay rise or anything like that, if I do well. Everything is quite clear in the contract, so there is no problem. I am relieved my problems are over. There was a lot of hassle over my contract but I knew I would win in the end. I sometimes had doubts if I would come to Celtic because of all this, but my managers kept telling me Celtic's interest remained strong.

"That was important to me. Other clubs said they were interested but only Celtic were strong enough to make a concrete offer. I hope I can bring a lot to Celtic and having worked with Wim for three months at Feyenoord, I know what a good trainer he is. I was impressed with the way Pierre van Hooijdonk improved when he came here. He was a good player when he came from Holland but not as good as he is now. I also hope to improve. Playing in front of 50,000 fans every home game will take a bit of getting used to but they made me feel very welcome and I hope I can help bring success to them. It's a great honour to sign for a club that are respected throughout Europe."

A newly-signed player stating that his new club are 'respected throughout Europe' more often than not can reek of PR spin-doctoring and is generally par for the course these days, a sort of verbal badgekissing routine that we had come to expect, especially at Celtic. The 'respected' bit may seem a bit soft for a team that has actually won the European Cup but also paradoxically hackneyed considering it had been 30 years since the triumph of the Lisbon Lions... But with Larsson remorselessly foraging up front like a ravenous she-cat intent on feeding kill after kill to her devoted family it wouldn't be long before Celtic were not only respected throughout Europe but once more feared throughout Europe.

Chapter II
Heroes For Hire
The Pretenders are dead. Long live the King

THE faithful devotees of Celtic Football Club need heroes like a fish needs water, ordinary players in ordinary teams starve us of the much-needed oxygen we require to get us through from game to game, season to season and decade to decade. The will to live wilts in those lacklustre periods of infertile listlessness when the production line of talent with that extra something dries up - but apathy never sets in. Indifference is an accusation that could never be levelled at Celtic supporters and it is when the chips are down, when all seems lost; at precisely the time one would expect apathy to proliferate like some contagiously fatal disease, that is when the concern multiplies. It's then that the unique empathy that Celts on the terraces have between each other and the Bhoys on the park rises to the surface. It bursts forth with a potency so invigorating that it galvanises green with white in a unique bond that has never, ever been broken. It has remained intact despite many trying times down through the decades and the 1990s produced more than their fair share of the dreaded blues for Celtic.

The empathy was perhaps naturally at its strongest with the 'heroes', the men who could deliver, those with that 'extra something' but what exactly is that vital ingredient that sets them apart? What is it that separates a no-hoper from an honest journeyman, an honest journeyman from a grafter, a grafter from a stalwart, a stalwart from a star and what elevates said star to the pedestal of an out and out superstar hero? Is it their skill, is it their long-term undying devotion to the club or is it something more aesthetic, something as simple as dreadlocked hair for example? The answer is, of course, all of the above and none of the above and if the solution is complicated then so be it - that is the reason why we don't have a conveyor belt manufacturing ready-made heroes on a seasonal basis. We have had players with undoubted skill, we have had players who have spent season after season with the club, we have had the badgekissers and we have had the pin-up personalities but there are examples of all of the above who have never made it to the rank of Celtic hero. Then there are the true Celtic heroes who possess various quantities of all of the above qualities - then there is Henrik.

Looking back at the late 1990s it's no easy task to work out who needed whom most. Did Henrik need Celtic more than Celtic needed Henrik? There's no doubt that after Larsson's dreadful Feyenoord episode he needed an injection of something to remedy the career-threatening disorder - but what? Could he not have received the vaccination to rid him of the post-Feyenoord syndrome elsewhere with another team? And what of Celtic - they needed a hero in 1997 and they needed one badly, but could they not have procured another player from another team? The answer to both questions, of course, is yes but, all the same, both would be casting their fates to the wind and we all know what happens when the wind changes direction. Larsson could have cured his ailment by moving anywhere, even back to Helsinborgs, although a move elsewhere in Europe may not have presented the same therapeutic balm he received at Celtic - we will never know. And Celtic? Although the club could have looked elsewhere, the '90s were riddled with tried and failed attempts at acquiring a bona fide champion for the supporters to idolise. The public parading of another new signing could yet turn out to be one more red herring for the fans to choke on a season or two down the line. So the answer to the 'who needed whom more' riddle is Celtic. It's simple, Celtic needed a hero but Henrik Larsson didn't need to be a hero.

It may not have been evident in July 1997 but Henrik Larsson was destined to become the latest in a long line of genuine Celtic heroes. If he had not come to Celtic he may not have achieved the same superstar status elsewhere but he would have survived. The question is, would Celtic have had the same survival instincts without him and would the remainder of the '90s and the early years of the new Millennium have been as successful without him? In a Celtic context, one of the qualities that sets heroes apart from the madding crowd is the ability, either on a regular or one-off basis, to put one over on Rangers. Even in these days of European competition and nights of glory under the Celtic Park floodlights, scoring a goal against, never mind masterminding the downfall of, Rangers can bestow on any player the eternal gratitude of everyone wherever the green is worn. A Celt who does the business against our oldest rivals gets extra brownie points with a gold star on top and immediately rises in the estimation and empathy stakes. Scoring against Rangers is one thing, winning a game against them is another, winning the championship is yet another but stopping Rangers from beating Celtic's historic nine-in-a-row milestone is way up on another sphere altogether and, for many, Henrik Larsson is the key ingredient in not only stopping the 10 but also in amassing the glittering array of trophies won since then.

Of course, Larsson is only one ingredient in the recipe that has tasted so sweet to the Celtic support over the last seven seasons but he really is the cream that sets the whole thing off and we all know that cream rises to the top. Not all of the ingredients blended together so tastefully during the 1990s however, and although some of them sated the appetite when fresh, they soon soured and left an unpleasant aftertaste. These were the three-minute heroes. They came, they saw, they copped out. They may have had their reasons for rescheduling their sell-by dates but the bottom line is they were missing one of the crucial constituents in the hero outline. They didn't have the longevity that will endear a Celtic hero to the masses forever, the staying power that lifts a player from the ranks of the nearly men to the stratum of the true Celtic icon. The opinion of the Celtic support may still be divided on, either individually or as a trio, the standing of the flashes of brilliance that zipped through our lives in the '90s but looking at the big picture, that's all they were, flashes that flickered and momentarily blinded us and by the time we had opened our eyes again they were gone. They fail to measure up in the big picture in question but maybe the assessment is a tad unfair when said big picture is a wide landscape of panoramic proportions ranging from the likes of Jimmy Quinn 100 years ago right through to Henrik Larsson. There are scores of characters in the heroic Celtic work of art and each have added their own brushstrokes to the masterpiece in their own fashion, but there is no doubt that Henrik Larsson has moved in from the sidelines to stand in the centre, shoulder to shoulder with the likes of Jimmy Quinn, Patsy Gallagher and Jimmy McGrory.

Celtic heroes are cast from a different mould and the mould is never broken or thrown away - just re-adapted for the next hero and passed on down the line. So Larsson does come from the same mould as Jimmy Quinn, Patsy Gallagher, Jimmy McGrory, Charlie Tully, Billy McNeill, and Jimmy Johnstone - all Celtic heroes in their own right and all very different players but they all had that certain something, that Celtic elixir that has been passed on to Larsson.

Of course, there were Celtic heroes before Jimmy Quinn joined the club in 1900 but he was probably the first to encapsulate the ultimate ethos and acquire the status of superstar - quite simply he was the 'Pride of Celtic'. His eminence was assured in the 1904 Scottish Cup final when, with Celtic 2-0 down against Rangers, he grabbed the game by the scruff of the neck and scored a hat-trick to bring the trophy back to Paradise. He went on to score 216 goals in 331 appearances before retiring in 1915 and claimed his own cherished place in the Celtic history books. Patsy Gallagher was born to be a Celtic hero. He was small and wiry but his emaciated build belied a bravery and a football skill that was unsurpassed in its day. He wore the Hoops from 1911 though to 1926 and scored 196 goals in 464 appearances, the most famous of which being the 1925 Scottish Cup final when he apparently beat the whole Dundee team before somersaulting into the net with the ball between his feet. Then there was Jimmy McGrory, simply the greatest goalscorer of them all and the man who produced more records than George Martin - 472 goals in 445 appearances (yes the figures are the right way round) between 1922 and 1937 just about says it all.

The massed Celtic ranks had the privilege of watching all these players in their prime, basically right through their whole careers, although something bizarre occurred in 1928 when manager Willie Maley tried to sell McGrory to Arsenal for the then massive fee of £10,000 but the striker simply refused to leave Celtic. The attempted, but thankfully aborted, sale of McGrory hinted that the powers that be at Celtic were not averse to selling their top attractions. And Jimmy Delaney was 'allowed' to go in his prime when he had the temerity to ask for a rise in his £2-a-week wages. Delaney played from 1933 through to 1946 and, discounting the war years, scored 73 goals in 160 appearances. Celtic supporters had seen many excellent players leave the club down through the years but losing Delaney then would be comparable to selling Larsson in season 2001/02 - just unthinkable. Delaney joined Manchester United and he wouldn't be the last top player to move down south at the peak of his career - a hero lost, the first of many and for many and varied reasons.

The arrival of the 1950s saw the advent of hero-worship reach new heights away from the football field. When Jimmy Quinn rose to prominence, heroes for the great British public effectively came from a very narrow band of selection, mainly those who had done their bit for the Commonwealth either on the battlefield or by colouring in more pink on the World Atlas. Through the decades, reaching the North Pole, conquering Everest and the four-minute mile all constituted hero-status for those involved - all pretty dull stuff really but football introduced the man-on-the-street hero. Not only could this new brand of hero be the guy next door, but he was also in the public eye week-in-week-out on a regular basis. He was readily available constantly and, more to the point, practically anyone could aspire to being a Quinn, Gallagher or McGrory; you didn't have to accept the King's shilling and fly the flag on a foreign field or spread the missionary word in Africa. Medals were still the benchmark for accomplishment but Scottish Cup and league championship gongs were edging out the likes of the Victoria Cross in this new variety of hero-worship. Through time the football stars were joined by another new breed, the adulation industry was diversifying and the new strain came into our lives via Hollywood; the man and woman on the street had a whole new batch of idols to venerate and aspire to.

The 1950s arrived and witnessed the dawning of another development in the hero business when Rock 'n' Roll burst on to the scene and the seeds of the word 'superstar' were first planted. Another new word that arrived in tandem with Rock 'n' Roll was 'teenager' and this new youthful breed demanded their very own heroes. The slicked back hair and swiveling hips of Elvis Presley were tailor-made for the teenage revolution but, ironically, the first real hero of the new generation was not this young Adonis with the Hollywood good looks; it was an overweight, balding 30-something with a kiss-curl and he went by the name of Bill Haley. And, ironically, the top Celtic hero of the decade was a small, chubby, balding man who didn't even have enough hair for the kiss-curl - Charles Patrick Tully. Charlie Tully looked as if he would have been more at home working in the local baker's shop than plying his trade on the football field but the Irishman was beatified at Celtic Park. He scored 47 goals in 319 appearances between 1948 and 1959 and it was once said of him that he was 'the greatest soccer import Scotland has had in years' a mantle he was to hold until a new revolution in the hero market some decades later.

The 1960s and everything that went with that decade saw hero-worship mushroom and explode to match the diverse Cultural Revolution. Television played no small part in creating new heroes and football wasn't excluded - so much so that a young lad from Belfast named George Best was christened 'El Beatle' by the Spanish press. Something was also stirring in Glasgow and the Celtic fans' empathy with their team was such that democracy kicked in and the whole team was afforded hero status. The Jungle regularly belted out a song that paid homage to the great Jock Stein and the 11 Lisbon Lions on the park to the tune of 'He's Got The Whole World In His Hands' - from 'He's got Ronnie Simpson, number one' right through the entire team with the last-line refrain 'He's got the best team in the land'. The Swinging '60s had well and truly flowered up but the Gallowgate was hardly Carnaby Street and Celtic fans would have to wait until the 1970s to have their own 'pop-star' hero with the emergence of a young kid called Kenny Dalglish. He had the trendy haircut, he had the pin-up looks and, more importantly, he had the tremendous skill to ensure that his posters would be pinned to the bedroom walls of both Bhoys and Ghirls in Celtic households throughout the country. Dalglish scored 166 goals in 320 appearances for Celtic and was another hero lost at the height of his career, sparking an eruption of discontent among the massed faithful.

Part of the problem was that previously under Jock Stein, Celtic supporters had been spoiled by the wealth of talent that not only reached their peak with Celtic, but they also stayed there until retirement or moving on with the best wishes of all in the autumn of their careers. The last big-name player to leave in the pre-Stein era was Paddy Crerand and there were echoes of both Jimmy McGrory and Jimmy Delaney in his departure to Manchester United in February 1963. Like McGrory, Crerand was Celtic-daft and didn't want to go, but like Delaney he was 'forced' or 'allowed' to leave due to boardroom influence. And the fact that Crerand and United were to lift the European Cup a year after Celtic meant that he was the only Parkhead departure of the '60s to challenge on at least a level footing with those who stayed. Celtic fans weren't used to seeing their favourites leaving to go on to 'bigger and better things', surely no club could be bigger than Celtic? But a combination of the board's reluctance to part with bigger wage packets, the inhibitive reflection of the old Scottish league set-up and the exposure of football down south ensured that more than a few furniture removal trucks would be heading down the M6.

Jock Stein had been masterminding a new breed to take over from the ageing Lisbon squad and this pride of Lion cubs that grew to fame as the Quality Street Kids included the precocious talent of Kenny

Dalglish, Danny McGrain, Lou Macari, George Connelly and Davie Hay. It was a squad that could have and should have not only continued Celtic's success at the top of the European tree but also taken the club's championship run way beyond the magical nine-in-a-row figure. That was not to be and the first seeds of doubt were sown when, almost 10 years to the day after Crerand left for Manchester United, Lou Macari took the same road to Old Trafford for a then Scottish record fee of £200,000. For a whole generation of Celtic fans this was the first time a hero had left while at the pinnacle of his career. But the question that has be asked is, if Macari had been persuaded to stay would Davie Hay have remained instead of moving to Chelsea in 1974? If Hay has stayed would that have influenced his great friend, the amazing but tragic talent that was George Connelly, to carry on with his Celtic career? That being the case, would Dalglish have been tempted by Liverpool in 1977 and would Celtic have carried on beyond nine-in-a-row if this squad had remained together? Could a bit of tact and diplomacy, not to mention common sense, have dictated the board's stance in dealing with Macari to stop the rot from setting in? It was not to be, and from the Quality Street Kids only the great Danny McGrain was afforded the Celtic hero's honoured badge of true longevity after scoring eight goals in 657 appearances between 1967 and 1987.

By the early 1980s Celtic were still not free of the wages/Scottish football/English football syndrome and another born and bred Celtic hero was on his way in the shape of Charlie Nicholas. Nicholas had taken over Dalglish's mantle of the pop-star Celtic hero with not only the haircut but the off-field lifestyle that attracted front-page headlines rather than the back-page column inches which had been the norm for Celtic stars in the past. In 1983 though, the bright lights of London attracted the young star and when Arsenal came calling he was off. But a new hero was just around the corner and if Danny McGrain provided some dependability to Kenny Dalglish's wanderlust then Paul McStay supplied the reliability and steadfastness to counteract the flamboyancy and itchy feet of Charlie Nicholas. The Maestro that was McStay came straight from the McGrain school of responsibility and fidelity but by the end of the decade Celtic were beginning to spread their wings and look abroad for heroes.

One defining aspect of the Celtic hero make-up was that, up until the advent of the 1990s, they had all come through the ranks at the club or had been plucked the environs of lower league clubs very early on in their careers. There were a couple of exceptions like those of Brian McClair and John Collins, who were already experienced footballers by the time they arrived at Celtic Park before moving on to 'bigger and better things'. However, both were dyed-in-the-wool Celtic fans and fully acquainted with what the club meant to the supporters and what it constituted to be a Celtic hero. The revolution that saw the influx of foreign stars to Scottish football had already begun by the time Celtic drafted in Dariusz Dziekanowski from Poland's Legia Warsaw in 1989 and in the striking role he had made the biggest impact on the club since the days when Charlie Nicholas was scoring goals for fun. But big Jacki's flirtation with hero worship at Celtic was fleeting and he played out his latter days at the club languishing in the reserves before moving down the ladder to Bristol City in 1992. As the decade wore on the foreign revolution was in full swing and in danger of spiraling out of control. Accusations were made that, since not all of the imports were top-drawer quality, the young talent coming through the ranks of Scottish football was being eroded due to clubs importing new faces with inflated wage demands rather than nurturing home grown talent. Due to their spending power though, the Old Firm on the whole were able to rise above such finger pointing and 1994 saw Celtic embark on the road to not only strengthening the team but to killing two birds with one stone by importing ready-made heroes from the continent.

The first such instance was Dutchman Pierre van Hooijdonk who arrived from NAC Breda in 1994 and immediately burst on to the scene to become the darling of the Celtic hordes. The following season he was joined by Portuguese star Jorge Cadete, who signed from Sporting Lisbon and this marked a sea change in Celtic's policy. Whereas the signing of van Hooijdonk could be regarded as hit and miss as he was a relative unknown from a smaller club, Cadete was already a tried and tested internationalist from a big club with a European pedigree. The following season Paolo di Canio arrived from AC Milan and the Celtic support felt like the cat that had ran away with all the cream. They were truly lapping it up now they had three bona fide heroes all displaying their extraordinary wares within the confines of one team, and expectations were at their highest for the first time since the centenary season of 1987/88. The hopes never came to fruition, though, and Rangers were still running away with title after title; all Celtic had to show for their entrepreneurship was a Scottish Cup win over Airdrie in 1995 when van Hooijdonk scored the wining goal. The return wasn't great and added to the disappointment was the fact that the 'Three Amigos', as they came to be known, all had their 'leetle problem' with Celtic and managing director Fergus McCann. Rightly or wrongly, it wasn't so much a case of heroes for hire as heroes for higher wages.

Celtic were still in a state of flux at the time and the departure of Tommy Burns as manager didn't help matters in the slightest. Davie Hay was installed as acting manager and Murdo MacLeod came in as reserve coach in Burns' absence until the arrival of Wim Jansen, when Hay was made assistant general manager to Jock Brown. While Burns was still manager, van Hooijdonk left for Nottingham Forest and things were not looking at all rosy with the remaining members of the trio. Di Canio refused to turn up for the pre-season tour of Holland and Cadete had faxed in a medical certificate explaining his absence from the Celtic squad. The Italian was soon on his way down south to Sheffield Wednesday and Cadete signed for Spanish club Celta Vigo - it could hardly be surmised that any of the three had immediately gone on to 'bigger and better things'. The suffering Celtic support had gone from the heights of ecstasy to the depths of despair in one fell swoop. They needed a hero. One who would display the skill and finesse of the departing trio, one who would have the fans bellowing from the stands and, most importantly, one who would stick to his guns and stay.

We may not have known it back in July, 1997 but Henrik Larsson was to fit the bill to perfection and fill the boots of all three departing superstars in all capacities. The future Celtic hero was born on September 20, 1971 in Helsinborg, Sweden to Eva Larsson and Francisco Rocha, a sailor from the former Portuguese colony of Cape Verde just off the west coast of Africa. The couple had met and set up home together with Eva's son Kim and soon young Henrik, named after his uncle Henrique back in Cape Verde, was born before younger brother Robert appeared on the scene. Francisco, like most doting dads, bought his young toddler son a football but little could he have know what was to transpire as the youngster waddled about with the ball at his feet. As Henrik grew up, he could hardly have picked a better role model than the great Pele as Francisco's love of the beautiful game rubbed off on his son. Along with older brother Kim and the younger Robert, he would play for hours practicing the game and, although he was never a great spectator of the game, he would study the Pele video he had as well as tuning into the English matches that were broadcast to Sweden every Saturday afternoon at four o' clock. Liverpool were among the big favourites with Kenny Dalglish, Kevin Keegan and Terry McDermott as well as Ossie Ardilles at Spurs catching the eye of the young Henrik. There were other attractions such as ice hockey, but although the youngster skated on the frozen ponds of the Swedish winter, football was the only thing for him. We've all had teachers asking us what we want to be when we grow up and the stock answer for most young boys is either train driver or fireman but Henrik always answered 'football player.'

By the time he was only six-years-old he was playing for Hogaborg BK and that only reinforced his dream to make football his career but his height and weight were conspiring against him. Things got worse when, at the age of 12-years-old, all his team-mates and classmates seemed to take a growth spurt while he remained lightweight and rather easily knocked off the ball. This was when his earlier penchant for always being in a rush and running everywhere paid off and his quickness and agility played a big part in his football style. At 13-years-old, he thought his dream was over as his bigger team-mates took to the field while he spent each game on the bench and his enthusiasm for the game was waning. He simply stopped trying, but coach Bengt Persson took the young Henrik aside and convinced him that he definitely had the talent to become a footballer but he had to start trying again. Bengt explained that Henrik would soon develop physically and grow but also that talent wasn't the be all and end all to becoming a great footballer - he would also have to work hard. Bengt's words of wisdom also included the shrewd counsel that dedication, not to mention luck, played massive parts in any footballer's career. It was that very advice which stuck with the young Henrik and it's a work ethic that he carries around with him to this very day. The talk with Bengt paid off as the 15-year-old Larsson was asked to train with the Hogaborg first team during the summer and the following season he joined them as a fellow senior. A year later he made his debut as a 17-year-old while still working as a fruit packer and supervising younger aspiring footballers at a youth centre, and he had turned the corner on to the road that would eventually lead to the East End of Glasgow and Celtic Football Club. And so it was that Henrik Larsson made his Celtic debut and while the Three Amigos instantly stamped their claim for hero status in the East End with inspiring debuts, the Swede hardly landed with his feet running when he came off the bench to replace Andreas Thom in the 57th minute of a league game at Easter Road.

Larsson was barely on the field when he teed up Hibernian's Chic Charnley for a screaming blockbuster of a goal and the Celtic fans could be forgiven for thinking what all the fuss was about in signing this guy who wasn't getting a game for Feyenoord. It was the most inauspicious of starts for the Swede, especially as the match ended in a 2-1 defeat for Celtic in the first game of the campaign when they had to stop the dreaded 10 from becoming a reality. To make matters worse, the unexpected source of the Celtic goal was defender Malky Mackay. Things didn't bode well not just for Larsson but also for new coach Wim Jansen, the team and the supporters at the start of what was a do or die season. Amazingly, as season 2003/04 dawned, Jackie McNamara was the only surviving member of the Celtic squad who welcomed Wim Jansen and Henrik Larsson seven years previously and he can still recall the trepidation at the start of the new season and the 'oh no, not again' feeling from the supporters at having yet another manager installed in such a short period of time.

McNamara recalled: "For me personally as a player, that was my first change of manager as Tommy Burns had signed me. But we were actually on the pre-season tour, with Murdo MacLeod taking the training at the time, and we were told that the new manager was coming while we were over there in Holland. That's when Wim came in and we first met him. Players obviously like to keep their place in the team but there was a general consensus among us that the team had to be strengthened. Of course, that was the case, not just because there was a change of manager but every year you have that period when people expect new signings with players coming in and going out, obviously more so with a new manager when he has to see what's there or someone has to tell him what he needs, and he has to find out what he wants as well. There was also the added threat of Rangers attaining 10-in-a-row, and that was a heavy a burden to bear. There was a tremendous amount of pressure, even on Tommy Burns while he was still here. The pressure Tommy was under before he left was incredible."

Of course, Henrik Larsson arrived along with other pre and early season singings such as Darren Jackson from Hibernian, Stephane Mahe from French club Rennes, Regi Blinker as part of the deal which took Di Canio to Sheffield Wednesday, Craig Burley from Chelsea, Marc Rieper from West Ham United and Jonathan Gould from Bradford City. So Larsson was just one of many potential Celtic heroes but McNamara's first impressions were good ones. "Obviously we knew Henrik was a good player, I remember watching him in the World Cup in America. He was just the guy with the dreadlocks, quick and he scored goals but when he first came we saw that he had good ability. The rest of the squad thought so as well. It was all good vibes, we knew he was a good player and obviously Wim had worked with him before and he knew what he was getting.

"I don't think we expected that the guy we got was going to turn out the way he did. We knew we were getting a good player but Henrik excelled way beyond that. It didn't seem that way when he passed to Chic Charnley at Easter Road. To be honest, I really didn't think much of it at the time. I remember Henrik talking about it, saying that it was a nightmare start for him in teeing Chic Charnley up, but the ball he gave away was 30 to 35 yards out; it wasn't like he lost the ball in the six-yard box. I remember thinking, and still do feel, that Henrik was a bit hard on himself, a bit over-critical. We knew it was a bad performance from the whole team and we were all pretty down anyway, as we didn't play well at all as a team in our first game of the term in what was a really big season for us

"He soon settled in, though, and practically right away we realised that he was something special. You could see he had it all, he was strong, quick and a great finisher. Great vision, he could see everything around the park, you noticed that in training, he's just one of those guys that got better and better. What sets him apart from other players is that I think he's an all-round player, he's got everything in the all-round game rather than just having the instincts of a penalty box striker. You know he will get you goals and he can set them up for himself as compared to a penalty-box striker, as we saw in the 6-2 match against Rangers when he made one of his goals out of nothing. He can provide, he can hold the ball up and he's strong. He can get headed goals from corners. There is just so much to his game and that makes him a top, top player."

McNamara should know as he has had to face the Swede in training and that gives him some inkling of what opposition defenders spend Friday night sweating about as they lie in bed trying to get some sleep before facing the charismatic Larsson. The current longest serving Celt said of his esteemed team-mate: "He's very difficult to play against in training. He's very strong and if you go in too tight he will just turn you and he's away from you. He's an intelligent player and his all-round game is difficult to play against. I certainly wouldn't fancy playing against him in a competitive game, not really, no. The closest I came was before Henrik arrived here and I played for Scotland at Ibrox against Sweden but Henrik was sub I think. I played right wingback in the first-half and Craig Burley came on for the second-half. But he is definitely difficult to play against. His pace isn't lightning but he's still quick. He's quick upstairs as well so he knows where the ball is coming from; he knows what's around about him. Most importantly he knows where the defender is, he knows when to hold the defender off, when to turn and when to lay it off. He was very important to us lifting the Championship that season and stopping 10-in-a-row. I thought he had a great season. He scored quite a lot of vital goals for us both away and at home. He obviously set us off on the last day against St Johnstone. He settled us down a bit with that tremendous goal when, very early on in the game, he bent the ball into the corner. That was very important. We could have done with another one right after it because it was getting a bit nervy towards the end of the game until Harald Brattbakk scored."

McNamara added: "He's very quiet away from the football field, very family orientated. He's very modest, not a big time player with the attitude that you sometimes see with a guy of his ability. He's very down to earth and I've always got on well with him. But the big question now is how much will Celtic miss him if and when he leaves. It's hard to even contemplate when you look at all his assets and what he had brought to the club since he's been here and he's been a joy to play with. You just know that when you put a ball up there in to his feet it's going to stay there and not come bounding back to you. Sometimes that's the difference when you've played with other strikers and it's a fight for a 50/50 ball. You know if you put a 50/50 ball to Henrik it's going to stick. You know he's going to do something with it or he's going to hold it up and you can get round him and that's something we've always had with him in the team. He's great to play with because he's very intelligent in his vision. He's very much a team player."

So at least, despite as Larsson says himself, "making Chic Charnley a big man in Scotland", the Swede's debut was out of the way and the following weekend he returned with the Celts to Edinburgh, Tynecastle being the venue this time. Hearts, however, were not the opposition. The occasion was a League Cup match and Berwick Rangers had switched their home tie from Shielfield Park to the capital and that is where a crowd of only 6,267 witnessed Larsson's first ever goal in Celtic's colours, the first of over 200 and the first time the soon-to-be famous tongue was on public view. Celtic romped to a 7-0 victory over the northern English side and it would be fair to say that the result wasn't exactly unexpected. So no-one was taking anything for granted or claiming that Celtic had bounced back from their opening day league defeat at Easter Road. However, a few days later, Larsson made his home debut when Dunfermline came visiting on league duty and if Celtic were hell bent on proving that they were worthy of stopping Rangers reaching 10-in-a-row, they were going about it in a very strange way indeed. The Pars triumphed 2-1 with the Celtic goal coming from an Andy Thom penalty and just 180 minutes into the new season, Rangers fans were already rubbing their hands in glee at attaining double figures. In midweek, Celtic visited Perth to play St Johnstone in the next round of the League Cup and the result, although a winning one, was far from satisfactory as a Simon Donnelly penalty was all that separated the teams, so Larsson had still to prove himself against Premier opposition.

That was to be rectified by the weekend when Celtic returned to McDiarmid Park to face the Saints again, this time on league duty, and the Celts at last picked up their first points of the season but only after Jonathan Gould had pulled off a wonder save. Just a minute before the half-time break, Larsson unfastened the home defence by scoring with a sublime header from a Donnelly cross to open his league account. Celtic won 2-0 with Darren Jackson netting the other goal. A few days later it was back to European duty for the Celts in the return leg of the UEFA Cup second qualifying round tie with Austrian side Tirol Innsbruck. An ineffective display in the away leg merited not much more than the 2-1 defeat Celtic returned home with. An Alan Stubbs goal to two Christian Mayrleb counters was all that Celtic had to show for their endeavours. Although stopping the dreaded 10 was definitely top of the must-do list for that season, European football was in Celtic's blood and the Bhoys on the park were going to have to draw on the rich vein of the club's traditional fighting values if they were to have any chance of progressing at the expense of the Austrians. It turned out to be one of those nights - for the first time that season the Celts managed to win a game in which the Celtic goal had been breached, it was a rollercoaster of a game which the Celts eventually won 6-3, it was the first time in European football that the Celts had lost five goals over two legs but still gone through, AND Henrik Larsson scored his first goal in front of the Celtic Park faithful. The Celtic goals were shared by Simon Donnelly and Craig Burley with two each, Morten Wieghorst and Andreas Thom - Larsson's first strike at Paradise was an own-goal so the jury was still out on him. Like the majority of own goals, it was unavoidable, an unlucky deflection and, with hindsight, maybe an unfortunate by-product of the striker's willingness to track back and help the defence, but such was Larsson's professionalism none of the above explanations would have made him feel any better. The only cure would be goals, and lots of them, at the right end of the field - and they were to arrive soon.

The cancellation of the Old Firm game scheduled for September 1 and international duty (Larsson wasn't selected for the Swedish World Cup qualifier with Latvia) ensured that Celtic's next action wasn't until September 10 in a home League Cup tie against Motherwell and eight minutes from the end, Larsson headed his first 'proper' goal in Paradise. After a fortnight of inactivity on the club front, this was the first game in a demanding glut of matches and, as luck would have it, Motherwell were the opponents come the weekend at Fir Park on league duty and a Craig Burley double and a Simon Donnelly single gave the Celts a 3-2 victory. Challenging as that game may have been, the next 90 minutes of football were set to provide a somewhat sterner test when Liverpool visited the East End of Glasgow in the UEFA Cup First Round proper. No-one gave Celtic much of a chance and the doubters appeared to be in the right when Michael Owen gave the visitors an early lead. However, wonderful strikes from Jackie McNamara and Simon Donnelly gave Celtic real hope until the final minute of the game when Steve McManaman hit the Celts with a sucker punch and the game finished 2-2. Just short of a 50,000 capacity crowd turned up the following Saturday to pay homage to their heroes and Birthday Bhoy Henrik Larsson celebrated his 26th in fine style by giving the Celtic crowd two presents and two clinical examples of what they could expect a lot more of in the future. He scored both goals in Celtic's 2-0 victory over Aberdeen but it was the execution of the goals that was to be a blueprint for many more. The first was a delicate clip while the second was an excellent dead-ball free kick, the first such conversion since the days of Pierre van Hooijdonk.

Larsson had arrived and the crowd were at last beginning to realise that they had the making of another Celtic hero - someone that could galvanise the efforts of the whole team and halt Rangers' march to No.10. The Aberdeen victory was followed by a 2-1 triumph over Dundee United at Tannadice and the opening two defeats to Hibernian and Dunfermline were cast to the wind as Jansen's men now looked the part, they were gelling together and for the rest of the season defeats would only be seen as momentary blips on an otherwise upward progress. The Celts still had that trip to Anfield to contend with, though, and came so close to seeing off the Liverpool giants. A goalless draw was fought out; Celtic emerged unbeaten but lost on the away goals rule so the European dream was put on the back burner for another season. On the league front, Kilmarnock (4-0), table-topping Hearts (2-1), St Johnstone (2-0) and Dunfermline (2-0) were all put to the sword, with Larsson scoring in each of the games including another double against the Rugby Park side. The victory over St Johnstone took the Celts to the top of the league. Then came a shock home defeat to Motherwell sandwiched between the first two Old Firm games of the season. The Celts lost the first of these 1-0 at Ibrox and having two 'goals' chalked off in the following Motherwell match just about summed up Celtic's luck, but they rallied somewhat in the second derby encounter with an Alan Stubbs last-minute goal taking a share of the points against Rangers at Celtic Park - a header that was to prove excruciatingly crucial as the season came to a climax.

The next game featured another Larsson brace at Celtic Park as Dundee United were defeated 4-0 in the first of a double-header against the Tangerines. The venue for the second meeting was Ibrox as the occasion was the League Cup final, staged there due to Hampden still being in the process of renovation. The Celts had beaten Dunfermline 1-0 in the semi-final at Ibrox thanks to a Craig Burley strike back on October 14 and the final was set for the last day of November. The Oasis anthem 'Roll With It' reverberated from the Ibrox stands and PA system as Wim Jansen urged his troops on to lifting the first piece of silverware available since he arrived as manager and the Bhoys came up with the goods. Danish defender Marc Rieper broke the deadlock in the 20th minute and just three minutes later, Larsson stamped his imprint on the game when his 20-yard shot scuffed Maurice Malpas before looping over the keeper and into the net. Craig Burley was to add another as the delirious Celts in the Ibrox stands partied to celebrate not just another League Cup triumph, but also the prospect of at long last turning the corner into a more affluent avenue - Championship Street.

Just three short months after discarding his Feyenoord nightmare to the out-tray by joining Celtic, Henrik Larsson held a cup-winners' medal in his hand, knowing that he had scored in the final and it was a sensation he wanted more of - and one that he was to experience again and again in the green and white of Celtic. The celebrations though, despite the League Cup bearing the Coca-Cola moniker, resulted in the half-expected cup hangover and when the Celts travelled to Rugby Park the following week to meet the then current Scottish Cup holders Kilmarnock, a dull 0-0 draw failed to provide the hair of the dog. They were soon back on the boil, however, with a 2-0 win over Aberdeen at Pittodrie with another Larsson goal, then, while Rangers drew 0-0 with Dunfermline, a 1-0 home win over Hearts who had reclaimed the top spot in the league. That was followed by a 5-0 trouncing of Hibernian at Celtic Park with yet another Larsson appearance in the goalscorers' list but the year ended with an unexpected 1-0 away defeat at St Johnstone. The final month of the year saw yet more development on the transfer front when Paul Lambert joined from Germany's Borussia Dortmund in a surprise move and striker Harald Brattbakk was drafted in from Norwegian side Rosenborg. The new forward's style was based on an explosive burst of pace and he was expected to form a Scandinavian strike force with his new Swedish partner up front but as the New Year dawned the goals were to come from an unexpected source.

The goals still arrived from the new intake but it was from the cultured play of midfielder Lambert rather than the fleet of foot Norwegian. The year 1998 opened with the traditional Old Firm first footing when Rangers came to Celtic Park but the statistic of a 2-0 win for the Celts thanks to goals from Lambert and Burley only begins to tell the whole story. The game marked a sea change and a shift of power in the goldfish bowl of Glaswegian football. The Celts totally annihilated

Rangers with a display over the entire 90 minutes that belied the scoring of only two goals. It was Celtic's first New Year victory over Rangers in a decade, it was the first in the league at Celtic Park since March 1994 and the first league win over the Ibrox side at all in over two-and-a-half years and 11 meetings. Celtic had lost only one goal in their previous eight domestic encounters and had lost only 13 goals in their 20 Premier League games so far that season. Following the high of the Old Firm victory there was another blip, this time coming in a 1-1 draw with Motherwell but it was Lambert once again who found the net, this time against his former club. Celtic then visited Tannadice and another 2-1 win was recorded over Dundee United before Larsson got on the scoresheet again the following week in a 3-1 home win over Aberdeen as the chase for the championship really boiled over in a three-way race. There was a ménage a trois at the top of the table with the razor thin division of goal difference separating Celtic, Rangers and Hearts - and Tynecastle was Celtic's next port of call.

The following Saturday, Rangers again drew with Dunfermline, this time 1-1 at Ibrox, and 24 hours later Celtic and Hearts took to the field in Edinburgh knowing that the victors would top the table that evening. Thanks to a Jackie McNamara goal, Celtic topped the league for a grand total of 47 minutes before a calamitous stramash in the final minute put paid to Celtic's hopes of being outright leaders. A Jose Quitongo shot ricocheted off the Celtic defence and fell at the feet of Neil McCann, his attempt came back off Rico Annoni and gifted Quitongo with another bite at the cherry, his second effort came off Stephane Mahe's arm and passed the helpless Jonathan Gould in goal. The top-of-the-table triumvirate was still in force with all three teams in stalemate. A week later Kilmarnock were the visitors at Celtic Park and Harald Brattbakk finally found his league shooting boots by firing in all four goals in the 4-0 trouncing of the Ayrshire side but Rangers beat Hibs while Hearts were also victors over Motherwell so the league impasse still held firm - but not for long. Brattbakk kept his shooting boots on for the next game when he scored two against Motherwell, while Larsson also found the net in the 5-1 home win over Dunfermline but it was the following round of league games that were to not only separate the top trio but also invite the peculiar, not to mention downright impossible beforehand, scenario of Celtic supporters cheering a Rangers goal.

On Saturday, February 28, Celtic travelled to the capital again, this time to Easter Road to play Hibs while Hearts bussed the opposite way along the M8 to play Rangers at Ibrox. The Celtic players and support well knew that if they did the business in Leith then the odds would shorten on them winning the league. Something had to give at Ibrox and Celtic would either top the league on their own or share top spot with whoever triumphed on the South Side of Glasgow - but just as long as Celtic won at Easter Road. This was one game where they just couldn't afford a slip. By then Hibernian had all but resigned themselves to playing First Division football the following season and, with everything to play for, Celtic were expected to walk all over the bottom-placed club. It wasn't to turn out as expected, though. It was another tense game in a season when nails were bitten to the quick. One solitary goal, drilled home by Marc Rieper, was all that separated the sides and even that was disputed by the Hibernian defence.

A Jackie McNamara corner was headed on by Larsson for Alan Stubbs to challenge home goalkeeper Bryan Gunn and the ball fell on the line. The ball was cleared by Jimmy Boco but only as far as the Dane who managed to keep the ball down and he fired home from 14 yards out. The Hibs defence questioned the legality of Stubbs' joust with Gunn but referee Jim McCluskey was having none of it. That goal arrived in the 25th minute and with Hibs playing deep, that gave the massive travelling Celtic support the opportunity to pay a bit more attention than usual to the live radio report beaming in from Ibrox. It wasn't all pipe and slippers stuff from the Celts, though, and a Barry Lavety shot was blocked by Stubbs on the line. If the Scouser hadn't been in the right place at the right time then the Celtic support's drinking bouts that night would have had an entirely different complexion. As it was, the news coming over the airwaves wasn't the worst. Hearts were leading 2-1 and if Celtic were going to share the top spot with anyone, the choice would be anyone other than Rangers. The Hibernian fans on the other hand obviously couldn't stomach seeing Hearts at the top of the tree, especially as the Edinburgh clubs would be book-ending the table with Hibs at the bottom. However, as the radio signals beaming in from Glasgow blurted out that Jorg Albertz hit a last-minute equaliser for Rangers, Easter Road erupted in a sea of green and white - at both ends. The Hibs fans obviously enjoyed the kick in the teeth for Hearts but the sight of any team's fans cheering a goal for their greatest rivals, never mind Celtic fans hailing a Rangers strike was a bizarre but highly memorable and enjoyable one to behold. After weeks of sharing top spot and being level on points with both Hearts and Rangers, Celtic at last unleashed the shackles of joint ownership - the lead was theirs and theirs alone.

There was no need for the radio mania the following weekend as the Celts were scheduled to play Dundee United at home on the Sunday and, 24 hours earlier, the events of Saturday afternoon made for a good day off from the office as Rangers lost at Motherwell while Hearts could only manage a 1-1 draw with Kilmarnock. The Celtic support rolled up to Paradise secure in the knowledge that victory would open up the gap further over the chasing pair. One thing the advent of live TV football and the introduction of 24-hour delays initiated is the acceptance that Celtic players and supporters need to don bulletproof boots on a Sunday for fear of shooting themselves in the foot. And so it transpired that the gap was widened but not by as much as we were hoping for when all the team could muster was a 1-1 draw with United. Next up was a 1-0 away win over Aberdeen at Pittodrie thanks to a Craig Burley penalty and the lead up to the following weekend was brimful of hope and expectation as Hearts were to be the visitors at Celtic Park. But Celtic failed to secure the three points they needed to lift themselves five points clear at the top. A thrilling but ultimately goal-less 90 minutes was played between the two title contenders as Rangers came back into the debate by winning at Dunfermline. Celtic were now just two points ahead of Hearts while Rangers sat another point below the Edinburgh side. There was, however, some brief respite from the hectic league schedule the following weekend, that is if a Scottish Cup semi-final against Rangers could in any way be termed as brief respite.

Although Harald Brattbakk didn't appear on the Premier League goalscoring charts until his quadruple against Kilmarnock back on February 21, he had indeed opened up his Celtic account a month earlier in the Scottish Cup. Celtic were first out of the hat and paired with Morton so the home team were fully expected to take care of the First Division Greenock side. Former Celt Billy Stark was then in charge of the Cappielow side just months after managing Celtic in their last three games of the previous season following the departure of Tommy Burns. Stark finished off the season by leading Celtic to two wins and a draw but even he had admitted that his new Morton charges would have to have their best day ever while Celtic experienced their worst ever if the Greenock team were to progress in the Scottish Cup. Morton just about held firm against the expected battering ram and a Brattbakk goal near the start followed by a strike from Darren Jackson near the end took Celtic through. An away trip to East End Park beckoned in the fourth round and the Norwegian was again on target, this time backed up by a rare Stephane Mahe goal to take Celtic through 2-1 against Dunfermline. The new Bhoy kept up his healthy Scottish Cup ratio in the quarter-finals against Dundee United at Tannadice in a game that truly went right down to the wire. Morten Wieghorst had added to Brattbakk's counter but the sides were level at 2-2 with the final seconds ticking away on the clock when a Swede put Celtic in front. It wasn't Henrik Larsson, though.

Celtic had earlier suffered and enjoyed a last-gasp winner at Tannadice when late goals, from Simon Donnelly and a deflected effort from Craig Burley, killed off the game after United had led for most of the match. This time Brattbakk struck early, his eighth goal in five games, but Kjell Olofsson hit back with a double to put the home side in front. Wieghorst brought Celtic back into the proceedings but, with Celtic defending desperately in the last 10 minutes, it was going to take something special to avoid a replay at Celtic Park. Larsson's speed was crucial in catching a Brattbakk pass on the bye-line and he whipped over a curling cross which the Norwegian just failed to reach. However, United's Swedish defender, Erik Pedersen stuck out his leg and with almost the last kick of the game turned the ball into his own net to send Celtic into the semi-finals for the 11th year running. A place in the final was not to be as the 2-1 victory by Rangers not only put the mockers on the Celts lifting the trophy, thanks to the League Cup win, Celtic were the only team who could possibly win the treble and they were continually proving that they had the squad and fighting qualities to do so. It wasn't to be and now Celtic and Wim Jansen could fully concentrate on stopping the 10.

As it happens, Rangers were also the league opposition penciled in for the following weekend but sandwiched between the Old Firm double header was a potentially hazardous trip to Rugby Park. However, amid a freezing, howling, rain-lashed gale, Larsson was on song again with the opener in a 2-1 win for Celtic. The Kilmarnock win teed up Celtic for the trip to Ibrox but the Scottish Cup strife was to carry on into this league encounter. On the day, thanks to their endeavours at Kilmarnock, Celtic were three points ahead on the 31-game mark but despite a recently rejuvenated Larsson, Celtic lost 2-0 and Rangers' bid for the 10 received a massive injection of life while Celtic fans started to make enquiries about emigration forms. It was still tight at the top and on the evening of Sunday, April 12, Rangers led the league by one goal - both sides had 66 points after 32 games played with four more games each to play, and Hearts had been unexpectedly beaten by Hibs in the Edinburgh derby. Motherwell were next on the agenda as they visited Celtic Park the following Saturday while Rangers travelled to Pittodrie on Sunday and the TV schedule granted Celtic the opportunity to nose in front and gain the psychological advantage. Celtic grabbed the bull by the horns and tore Motherwell to shreds with a 4-1 victory featuring doubles by Donnelly and Burley - but only after the Fir Park side had the temerity to take the lead. Elsewhere, St Johnstone travelled to Tynecastle and held Hearts to a draw, meaning the Edinburgh side were now six points off the trail. And the Sunday afternoon TV viewing brightened things up even further when Aberdeen defeated Rangers 1-0. Celtic were now three points in front but the following weekend's outcome wasn't quite so rosy as Celtic dropped two points in drawing 0-0 with Hibernian at Celtic Park while Rangers defeated Hearts 3-0 at Tynecastle. Celtic now had their noses in front by only a single point and the 10 was still on.

The following week the roles were reversed with Rangers entertaining Kilmarnock on the Saturday while the Celts travelled to East End Park to face Dunfermline for the Sunday's TV game. A home victory for Rangers would give them a two-point advantage in real terms but the psychological benefit to them would be immeasurable and if Celtic didn't win at Dunfermline they could more or less say goodbye to their championship hopes and hello, hello to Rangers winning the 10. A Rangers win over the Ayrshire side was fully expected and even as the game dwindled to a close with the score at 0-0, a point would have Rangers on level pegging with Celts - even if only for 24 hours. The seconds continued ticking down, Celtic fans sat with their ears glued to the radio just hoping against hope that Rangers wouldn't score - then it happened - it's a wonder that there hasn't been an Ally Mitchell CSC formed in honour of the climax to that game - with the last kick of the match, Ally Mitchell not only put the ball in the Rangers net but he also slam-dunked it firmly right back in Celtic's court - all Celtic had to do was score more goals than Dunfermline and the league was theirs, the curse of the 10 would be banished from the very souls of Celtic supporters the world over. But Celtic, aided and abetted by a couple of dodgy refereeing decisions and a goal that hardly came from the textbook, not only shot themselves in the foot, they blew both feet to smithereens with a Magnum while the champagne magnums were kept on ice.

Simon Donnelly fired Celtic ahead 10 minutes before half time and the title party started to hot up but two disputed refereeing decisions involving Henrik Larsson were to have a grave impact on the game. When the Swede was clearly fouled in the penalty box, referee John Underhill failed to point to the spot but the main turning point came just seven minutes from the end. An innocuous-looking free kick was awarded against Larsson 40 yards out from the Celtic goal, the ball was punted into the box where Pars substitute Craig Faulconbridge rose to meet it with a looping mistimed header which was apparently going nowhere until it went over Jonathan Gould and into the corner of the net. The party was cancelled - at least for a week. The mathematics were simple. If Rangers won against Dundee United at Tannadice on the last day of the season then Celtic had to win over St Johnstone in their final 90 minutes - even a draw would mean that a three-goal victory for Rangers would see the title staying at Ibrox for the 10th successive year. On May 9, 1998, the stage was set for a finale to beat all finales as the Tannadice game was beamed back to big screens at Ibrox where the crowds would wait for their returning heroes who were being flown back in a helicopter specially chartered for the occasion - all they had to rely on was Celtic slipping up against St Johnstone, but they didn't count on Henrik Larsson.

At 3.00pm the 90-minute countdown started. At 3.02pm Larsson pounced and set the clocks back 10 long years to when Celtic had last lifted the title. He drifted in from the left before unleashing a magical shot that Alan Main had no chance of reaching and Paradise erupted as it had never done before - surely there were more goals to come after this exceptional early salvo from the Swede. We waited though; it was a long, long wait. The news came through from Tannadice that Rangers were 2-0 ahead and although Celtic were controlling the proceedings, there was still the chance, as George O'Boyle had earlier shown, that the

Saints could turn sinners by grabbing an equaliser. We waited and still we waited. At 4.28pm we waited no more - it had happened. Celtic captain Tom Boyd passed to Jackie McNamara on the right wing, he squared the ball in to the on-running Harald Brattbakk and the 10 was well and truly consigned to the realms of the twilight zone.

There was no 10. No 10-in-a-row. Never would a one-in-a-row championship run be so celebrated. In an inverted paradox this title win was just as important as any of the original nine won by Jock Stein's Celts in 1966 that started the whole shebang in the first place. Celtic supporters throughout the world celebrated as they had never celebrated before and parties went on well into the following week before abating. The Celtic players celebrated but Henrik Larsson may have taken time out for a quiet moment of contemplation away from the hubbub of activity all around him. Just 10 short months earlier he was going through a living hell and now he had a League Cup winners' medal and a Scottish Premier League Championship gong. He was the club's top scorer with 19 goals, 16 of them in the league. In four of his 35 league appearances his goals had been vital, the difference between three points for a win and one for a draw. The teeing up of Chic Charnley and the own goal for Tirol Innsbruck were forgotten - as were the Three Amigos. Another true Celtic hero was among us, and one of us. The legend was born.

Chapter III
Speaking in tongues
Normal service will be resumed after the break

SO within 10 months of signing on with Celtic, Henrik Larsson had won as many medals as he had done in his entire four years with Feyenoord and after nine years of torture the Celts weren't all that far away from lifting a treble under Wim Jansen. Still, we had stopped the 10 and that was the main thing - that was the only thing. Midfielder Craig Burley had won the Scottish Football Writers' Player of the Year award, the first Celt to earn the honour since Paul McStay had done so a whole 10 years earlier amid the centenary magic of 1988. Similarly, Jackie McNamara had lifted the Scottish Professional Footballers' Player of the Year accolade, carrying on from Paolo Di Canio's win the previous season while the term before that, McNamara had won the Young Players' award. The squad had been strengthened and Jansen had formed a Championship-winning side from the bare bones of a losing team. In season 1996/97 the Celts finished a full 15 points behind their oldest rivals as the Ibrox side reached the number nine figure. Jansen had turned that around at the first time of asking and there was no reason why the squad couldn't be strengthened further - or was there? Any outsider would be forgiven for thinking that everything in the garden was rosy but there had been trouble simmering under the surface throughout the majority, if not the entirety, of that winning season. Every silver lining has a cloud and this dark and broody smog almost threw a black veil over the joy of stopping the 10 as just two days after leading Celtic to the Premier League Championship, Wim Jansen resigned.

On Saturday, May 9 as the players and their kids wildly cavorted about the Celtic Park pitch in celebration of the historic title win, Wim just calmly strolled about with his hands deep in his pockets regarding the whole scene in a contemplative frame of mind. Were those hands thrust deep in his pockets thumbing some hastily-written notes explaining his resignation and was he reconsidering - don't put your mortgage on it. It's more probable that Wim had long decided that he had endured enough and winning the Championship, not even stopping the 10 was going to make him change his mind. Call it what you like, throwing in the towel, scuttling away from a sinking ship, looking a gift horse in the mouth or leaving Celtic in a lurch - there are no two ways about, Wim Jansen felt he was doing the honourable thing by leaving when he did. The roots of the whole problem were reasonably simple - it takes two to tangle. There was conflict in the job description parameters between him and general manager Jock Brown and that conflict became personal. They just didn't get on and rarely spoke two words together and Jansen felt his position was untenable. He had decided to go at the top; despite the lure of leading Celtic into another season defending the championship they had shed blood, sweat and tears to win. And as the parties all over Scotland and Ireland were still in full flow celebrating the historic win, the news broke that Jansen was leaving. Something had to give but the supporters just didn't want it to be Jansen - and neither did the players.

There was a fellowship in that squad; a camaraderie in the dressing room that belied the antagonism that permeated a couple of flights upstairs in Celtic Park's South Stand. The only problem was that Jansen had to flit between both floors and he wasn't prepared to sit halfway up or halfway down the stairs. The middle landing was not the place for a coach of his calibre. There was another problem for the players, though. In the dog-eat-dog world of professional football, their reasons for wanting Wim to stay needn't have been totally magnanimous, they would also have to prove themselves to the new manager and the batch of players recently brought in by Jansen would possibly feel in a particularly precarious position. Aside from Henrik Larsson, the new intake included Regi Blinker, Harald Brattbakk, Craig Burley, Jonathan Gould, Darren Jackson, Paul Lambert, Stephane Mahe and Marc Rieper. However, Larsson may have been wondering if he had the Sword of Damocles hovering dangerously once more above his head. Was his Celtic dream about to evaporate and mirror the Feyenoord nightmare? After all, was he not initially happy when Wim Jansen signed him for Feyenoord before the coach left, eventually leaving Larsson at the mercy of a manager who would be his undoing? Was there a chance, however remote, that the spectre of Arie Haan would come back to haunt him in the shape of another coach who just didn't rate him?

Any fears of that sort from any of the players were allayed when the new man for the Parkhead hot seat was introduced on Friday, July 17, 1998. Doctor Jozef Venglos was a football man and a fair man through and through and right away Larsson must have perceived that there were little if any similarities between the genial Slovak and the tyrannical Dutchman who had made his life a misery. Of course, players would leave over the course of the coming season; Simon Donnelly and Phil O'Donnell went to Sheffield Wednesday, David Hannah returned to Dundee United, Malky Mackay also travelled down south to Norwich, Brain McLaughlin went to Tannadice and Darren Jackson signed for boyhood heroes Hearts. Of that batch, Darren Jackson was the only player who had joined the previous season but he had joined on July 12, just prior to Jansen's arrival and, ironically and unwittingly, he was the reason for the first contretemps between the new coach and Jock Brown when Jansen had hardly had his feet under the table for five minutes. Obviously Jansen hadn't seen Jackson play, he hadn't seen any of the squad play, and when quizzed, Brown announced to the press that the coach had seen the player on video. The problem was that Jansen hadn't yet watched the tape and the brouhaha had begun - from little acorns....

Still, the Celtic players and their supporters could at least look forward to the new season with renewed vigour after halting the dreaded 10 and they started the season as champions when the flag was unfurled in the newly revamped stadium which now had a capacity of over 60,000. The enmity over the close season goings on were not easily forgotten by the fans, though, and there was jeering from the stands when Fergus McCann unfurled the green and white Saltire acknowledging the 1997/98 achievement of Wim Jansen. But any off-field animosity didn't make it on to the pitch as the Celts started the defence of their title in fine fettle with a crushing 5-0 victory over Dunfermline thanks to a Burley hat-trick, a goal from Simon Donnelly and Malky Mackay repeating his feat of scoring in the opening league game of the season. Larsson may not have found the net on that occasion but Celtic had earlier kicked-off in the Champions League qualifiers. A 0-0 draw with St Patrick's Athletic was played out in Glasgow and just days before the Dunfermline curtain raiser, goals by Larsson and Brattbakk delighted the Celtic fans in Dublin who witnessed Celtic going through 2-0 to meet Croatia Zagreb in the next round. Darren Jackson hit the only goal of the home tie and the Celtic fans were to first come across a name that would soon become very familiar - Mark Viduka.

However, by the Saturday, Larsson was back to doing what he does best by netting a double, one of them a penalty, at Pittodrie but the Aberdeen side won 3-2 in a topsy turvy game that left the punters scratching their heads in amazement. Celtic had scored an own goal, had Darren Jackson sent off and missed TWO penalties, Donnelly and Burley were the culprits, before Larsson netted his spot kick in injury time. Things obviously weren't going to plan for the new manager and the outlook worsened a few days later when Airdrie knocked the Celts out of the League Cup with a 1-0 scoreline. The home side's goal came from the penalty spot while Larsson was away on international duty with Sweden. The weakened Celtic side was also missing Brattbakk who was away with Norway, plus Marc Rieper and Alan Stubbs were sidelined through injury, but there were still no excuses for the Celts losing their grip on the trophy won under Jansen to the First Division side.

The Celts got back on the league track with a 2-1 home win over Dundee United but the following midweek failed to build on their 1-0 European advantage over Croatia Zagreb and went down 3-0. Hindsight throws up the reasonable argument that the next batch of league games lost Celtic the crown they had fought so hard to win - Dundee (1-1), Kilmarnock (1-1), Rangers (0-0), St Johnstone (0-1) and Hearts (1-1) - not a win in five games, the majority of them against teams that were ripe for the taking. On UEFA Cup duty, Celtic had beaten Portuguese side Vitoria Guimaraes 2-1 both home and away, with Larsson finding the net in the away leg, during that period but it was clear something was missing - goals. And Larsson was soon to remedy the situation with an amazing scoring run that was to truly hoist him up the pecking order of Celtic heroes, and people around Europe would soon begin to sit up and take notice.

Strange as it may seem now, Larsson was not yet the household name he is now and even Paul Lambert, who joined Celtic midway though the previous season from Borussia Dortmund admitted ignorance of the goalscoring machine who was setting Celtic and Scottish football alight. Lambert recalled: "To be honest I never knew him, I'd never heard of him, nothing like that. When I came to Celtic the only ones I really knew were the Scottish guys. There was absolutely nothing in the German press and I heard nothing in the Scottish camp on international duty. Because my life and my football were in Germany the only things I obviously missed from here was my family, that's all. I didn't miss anything else and if I'm being honest I didn't look at anything or hear of anything. So I never really knew him or heard of him or anything like that but obviously when I got to play with him we became friends and that's how it took off."

Despite all the trepidation surrounding the whole season, Lambert and the rest of his team-mates didn't even question the doubts over stopping the 10. "The thing was that we had to it." he said, "I mean everybody you met was saying you must stop it, you must stop it. And to do it with the team that we had and the amount of players that we used at that time was a phenomenal thing. It really was something to have done because we only used so many players and it was a team just built together within one year. To be fair, Wim was great. With his football knowledge allied with the players that he brought to the club, we managed it. And it's not an easy league to win by any manner of means because I thought Rangers were really strong at that time as well. Their tails were up and they were going for it so it was an amazing achievement to have won it - fantastic.

"And obviously Henrik played a massive part in winning the championship and stopping the 10. You just try your best but you know when he's got the ball he'll very, very rarely give it away and that's always the same because people think the simple things are nothing. But he does the simple things really well which is good for us. To play with him up front has been absolutely first class. He makes life easier for midfielders like myself. I think when you play with any top player the game becomes a lot easier for yourself and individuals as well as the team. He definitely makes it easy because you know when he's got it that things can happen. Even in the box you know that if he gets a chance he is going to score. And he will also track back and help in midfield, which is another massive help. He's a worker and I always think the best players in world, any or whatever top player you care to talk about, will work the hardest. People think the ability just comes and it's just a natural thing but you've got to really work hard to get it. His input to the entire team as a whole is immense, you need everybody to pull their weight and that's what people tend to forget. Even though he's a great player he works very hard for the team."

The midfielder added: "Fitness is a big part of his game and as to the combination ratio of skill and fitness in his game ... Wow! Both are high. To be fair, in the modern game you have to have so much fitness.

It's an important part of the game and allied to his ability it makes him a top player and nobody can deny that, but he's a fit boy. Now that he's 32 he won't feel any different than he did four or five years ago. His work-rate on the pitch is amazing. It's what you expect anyway from every player but it is never in question with him. You know you're going to get everything from him, which is good. But as for comparing him to other strikers in my career, I've played with great strikers. I've played with really great world-class strikers and he's definitely up there without a shadow of a doubt. But I don't like comparing and I won't compare Henrik with Karl Heinz Riedle, Stephane Chapuisat, Jean-Pierre Papin or players like that. And I won't compare because they are all individuals and all top, top players. But I wouldn't mind having Henrik playing up front ahead of me in a Scotland shirt. It would be great because in the national team we have many good players but we haven't got that predator instinct which he has, and if we could get a striker like that he definitely would be worth his weight in gold for the national team.

"When he was out with his broken leg it was a major thing; not just losing him but to lose any player to a broken leg is a low point as it's a severe injury. That happened but we didn't do enough throughout the season anyway to win the league or get anywhere near it that year. It takes a certain sort of character to come back from an injury like that. You have to be strong mentally and I think that is a big thing. Henrik and Stan Petrov were the same, both injured and both came back with the same mentality. I've had a few injuries myself, but touch wood, the only things I've had are stress fractures and things like that. But in football you've got to have a strong character to come through a lot of injuries and, to be fair, he actually probably came back better. That may sound a silly thing to say but he actually came back a better player. That says a lot for the type of character Henrik is and he still has that winning instinct away from the pitch. We play golf a lot and things like that and obviously the competitive edge is still there. But he's quiet, I find him quiet. He's a private person and I find, at this particular club anyway, you've got to be kind of quiet because you're in the limelight enough as it is and you don't need to go out and attract it. Celtic will miss him when he does go. In my opinion he is irreplaceable. You can't replace that goalscoring. You might do it, and touch wood somebody comes along and is able to handle it. But they've got to come and handle the whole club, handle themselves in this environment and that's not an easy thing. I think we'll do well to replace him for a few years to come anyway."

Lambert was on the scoresheet when Celtic got back to their winning ways after that five-game run with no victories to speak of but the other scorer in the 2-1 win over Motherwell was Harald Brattbakk, Larsson still wasn't finding the net. The next clutch of games did little to enhance his reputation as a striker either, Dunfermline (2-2), FC Zurich (1-1), Aberdeen (2-0) and Kilmarnock (0-2). But starting in November and going though the next 19 games until mid-March of the following year, he was to go on an absolutely astounding goalscoring spree that would leave all others standing in his wake. In only three of those 19 games would he fail to find the net and he would score an amazing 28 goals during that period, including three doubles, three hat-tricks and a quadruple. Larsson was on fire and the rest of Scottish football was feeling the heat with more than one experienced keeper getting his fingers burned as the Swede lit the touch paper.

Bookies around the country were also feeling the pinch as gleeful punters stuck a few bob on Larsson finding the net and the odds the Swede coming up with the goods shortened to almost miniscule proportions. The first of those goals unfortunately arrived in a 4-2 away UEFA Cup defeat at the hands of FC Zurich to halt Celtic's European intentions for that season. But the next game was something else altogether, and not just for the fact that Larsson banged in the first of several hat-tricks that season. In the weeks leading up to the game, Celtic signed a 33-year-old Slovak player from German side MSV Duisburg for just £300,000 - the unknown was called Lubomir Moravcik. Nobody was expecting much, especially the press, but on November 7, 1998, an unfortunate Dundee side were unlucky enough to be the visitors that would bear the brunt of a Celtic side inspired by the Slovak's mastery.

Celtic ran amok that day, with Moravcik and Larsson grasping the roles of main instigators in piling the pain on Dundee as Mark Burchill with two goals and Simon Donnelly with another put the icing on a magnificent 6-1 victory. The elation was tarnished somewhat a week later when a trip to Perth yielded a 2-1 defeat although Larsson had netted the solitary Celtic goal. But the big test was yet to come as Rangers were to visit Celtic Park on the following Saturday and questions were being asked, especially considering the McDiarmid Park defeat, of Moravcik's ability to turn it on against the big guns in the heat and fervour of an Old Firm derby. To be fair though, the same questions could have been asked of Larsson. For, despite his goalscoring prowess and the hero worship festooned on him by the Celtic faithful, the Swede had still yet to score against our oldest rivals despite no fewer than six attempts at trying. All questions were duly answered though on November 21, 1998 with more than a hint of subdued arrogance as Celtic simply tore Rangers apart by recording their biggest win over the Ibrox side since January 3, 1966.

Question1: Can Moravcik do it against Rangers?
Answer: Yes - proof, two goals.
Question 2: Can Larsson do it against Rangers?
Answer: Yes - proof, two goals.

Mark Burchill added another in a quite exhilarating 5-1 win that was as utterly enjoyable as it was unexpected. Larsson had ticked off another box, the only blank box left, on the true Celtic hero criteria list but it wouldn't be long before the ticks would be obscured - Larsson's personal list would eventually have more gold stars than an American Field Marshall's chest. The fanatical Celtic support had waited more than 30 years for a victory of such resounding magnitude and deep down they knew another three decades would probably pass before they had the opportunity to witness that sort of extermination job, a Demolition Derby, again - or then again, maybe not...

The following week, Motherwell were the visitors and Larsson was again on the scoresheet with, this time, Phil O'Donnell supplying the other in a 2-0 victory. There was a slip up seven days later, though, when another O'Donnell goal was all Celtic had to show for a 2-1 defeat by Hearts at Tynecastle, but while Larsson was on the ball in the next game at Tannadice only one point was gained in the 1-1 draw with Dundee United. Celtic needed a tonic and that arrived in almost a carbon copy of the Old Firm game when Dunfermline visited the East End of Glasgow. A 5-0 score was recorded with Larsson and Moravcik getting another double each, the other coming from Larsson's fellow Swede, and recent arrival, Johan Mjallby. Dens Park was the next port of call and Larsson led the way again and was joined on the scoresheet by O'Donnell and Norwegian Vidar Riseth.

The New Year beckoned with Celtic first-footing at Ibrox but sadly there was to be no repeat prescription of what Dr Jo ordered in the previous meeting. A 2-2 draw wasn't the worst outcome, though, and this time Alan Stubbs joined Larsson in netting the goals. Scottish Cup action was next on the agenda with Airdrie failing to repeat their earlier League Cup shock over Celtic. Larsson, O'Donnell and an own goal by the Diamonds' player-coach Sandy Stewart accounted for the 3-1 scoreline. Harald Brattbakk stole the limelight in the next match as St Johnstone came to Parkhead, with the Norwegian firing in a hat-trick to join Larsson and Moravcik in the scoring honours in the 5-0 debacle. Then Hearts were put through the Larsson mill as another hat-trick from the talismanic Swede racked up another three points and a 3-0 home win.

A few days later the Scottish Cup was back on the schedule and Larsson simply carried on with where he left off against Hearts - another hat-trick for the striker, with Brattbakk taking the score to 4-0 against Dunfermline. Kilmarnock were next up in the league and although they subdued Larsson, they didn't pay enough attention to Vidar Riseth and the Norwegian defender nicked in with the only goal of the game. Larsson made amends in the midweek match against Motherwell at Fir Park as Celtic went to town.

On a night of fiesta football Celtic hammered the Lanarkshire side 7-1, with Larsson netting FOUR of the goals. Moravcik, Burley and Burchill got the other but there was a price to pay in losing the Slovak to a hamstring injury. Dundee United were the next visitors to Celtic Park and in opening the scoring in the 2-1 win Larsson reached the glorious Golden Goal figure of 50. His 51st goal was in the Scottish Cup against Morton but he was joined on the scoresheet by a new name scoring his first goal in the same game, Mark Viduka had joined from Croatia Zagreb and another potential hero was added to the list. Larsson kept up the heat with another two against Aberdeen at Pittodrie in a 5-1 win, with a Viduka double and a Craig Burley goal making up the tally. There were, however, only another three Larsson goals to come in the seven Premier League and two Scottish Cup games that remained that season.

Celtic drew a blank in a 0-0 draw with Kilmarnock at Rugby Park but Larsson was back on the mark again with another double as the Celts defeated Dundee 5-0 at Celtic Park. Scottish Cup action called again as Celtic triumphed 2-0 over Dundee United in their 12th successive semi-final and the Celts followed that up with a 4-2 league win over Hearts. Larsson's 37th and final goal of the season came from the spot and proved to be the winner in a 1-0 home win over Motherwell. Celtic's next league action was a disappointing 1-0 defeat in Perth to St Johnstone and the frustration wasn't purely down to just losing three points. That result meant that the following weekend's Old Firm clash wasn't just a six-pointer; if Rangers won they would take the title - at Celtic Park. It goes without saying that chaos reigned that day and referee Hugh Dallas played his part in the proceedings.

The record books record a 3-0 win for Rangers but that hardly begins to tell the whole story. Celts Stephane Mahe and Vidar Riseth were sent off amid crowd trouble, mini pitch invasions and the man in black being hit with a coin. To make matters worse, the Rangers players idiotically mimicked the Celtic Huddle at the end of the game to spark even more violence in a city where the police were already assured of a busy night.

The final three league games could be considered pretty meaningless but try telling that to the 60,000 who turned up for the final home game against Aberdeen regardless. All that was left was the Scottish Cup, but that too was to prove a damp squib as an uninspiring final presented not only a 1-0 win to Rangers but also the domestic treble. However, although a team player like Larsson would never admit it, the season could be termed as a personal triumph for him and the fans knew they had a winner in the goalscoring stakes. He stuck away 37 that season and in the 30-odd years since Celtic lifted the European Cup, only four Celts had scored more in a season; Bobby Lennox 1967/68 (41), Kenny Dalglish 1972/73 (41), Charlie Nicholas 1982/83 (48) and Brian McClair 1986/87 (41). He truly was mixing it with exalted company and if his history of improving goals ratios was to continue then we could hope for even more in season 1999/2000 - that was in the lap of the gods, though, and the rays of sunlight from the heavens were not to shine too brightly on Celtic or Henrik Larsson that dark and grim season.

A Celtic close season in the 1990s just wouldn't have seemed like a Celtic close season in the 1990s without Celtic looking for a manager and in the summer of 1999 that's exactly what we got - a Celtic close season in the 1990s with all the usual thrills, frills, bills and ills. Dr Jozef Venglos decided enough was enough and called it a day and the seemingly annual summer media speculation gathered momentum once more.

In the 1990s, Celtic had widened their horizons and opened up the options in their quest to find a suitable manager after Billy McNeill was sacked in 1991. It was then that they abandoned the policy of only using former Celts when Liam Brady was installed as the new man. Brady was a Republic of Ireland hero and well acquainted with what it meant to be a Celt so there was no problem there. He was, however, untried as a manager and there was speculation as to his potential for the job - his tenure was not a success. Former Celt Lou Macari was next in October 1993 but his occupancy was the shortest yet and another Celtic hero in the shape of Tommy Burns came in. He held the reins until the arrival of Wim Jansen in 1997. The arrival of Jansen heralded the first appointment of a manager who had no previous emotional ties with the club but this time, unlike Brady, he was tried and tested in the managerial market.

The same could be said of the next selection in the shape of Dr Jozef Venglos but, like the Dutchman, his stay was only one short season. This is when Celtic adopted the belts and braces approach by taking out the insurance policy of having a co-pilot ready at the helm. The new manager was Liverpool and England legend John Barnes but his appointment came in tandem with, and at the behest of, the new director of football, Kenny Dalglish. The 'Dream Team', as the partnership was christened, were paraded in the summer of 1999, and although Barnes was young at 35-years-old and completely untested as a manager, with the Celtic hero that was Dalglish there to lend a helping hand, the expectations were high and mighty. However, it was only a matter of time before the belts and braces strategy went awry, Celtic's trousers still fell down - and in public.

Larsson was now working with one of those heroes he watched as a young kid back in Sweden when the old English First Division games were beamed into to his living room. There was the usual flurry of pre and early season transfer activity with the new faces featuring Israeli Eyal Berkovic from West Ham, Russian keeper Dmitri Kharine from Chelsea, an unknown Bulgarian youngster named Stilian Petrov from CSKA Sofia, Dutchman Bobby Petta from Ipswich Town, Brazilian Rafael Scheidt from Gremio and Olivier Tebily from Sheffield United all eager to please the newly installed manager. And, in the beginning, before the belts and braces buckled to bare Celtic's embarrassment, the dream seemed to be going to plan as a healthy run of wins were racked up by the Celts. Much of the early success was down to Larsson, who not only maintained his traditional habit of increasing his goals ratio, he also upped the ante and stepped on the gas full pelt with a mesmerising exhibition of goalscoring at its best.

The previous season he finished top scorer with 37 goals and by the end of October that term he had scored five of those goals in 18 matches. As season 1999/2000 unfolded he amassed an amazing 12 goals in only eleven matches during the same time period. Football pundits were scratching their heads in bewilderment as to just how many goals the Swede was actually going to end up with by the end of the season. That was something we can only surmise upon now, as fate intervened to ensure that Larsson would not see out the season and decreed why the month of October is the only possible barometer for measuring his improved goals ratio.

For on October 21, 1999 in the French town of Lyon, Larsson suffered the horrific leg-break that would send shivers down the spine of the millions who watched it on television and saw the frightening photographs in the newspapers. God only knows what those who were first on the scene felt and only Larsson will truly know how he suffered in pain that October night.

That all seemed so far away when Celtic, with the Dream Team at the helm, stormed to a 5-0 win over Aberdeen at Pittodrie on the first day of the season. Larsson got in on the act with two goals, as did Mark Viduka, with the other counter coming from Mark Burchill. Larsson wasn't on target in the first home game of the season but Celtic won 3-0 against St Johnstone nonetheless and the next port of call was Wales in the UEFA Cup. Lowly Cwmbran Town were the opposition and they capitulated 6-0 with Larsson hitting yet another brace. There was a blip at Tannadice the following weekend when the Celts went down 2-1 to Dundee United but that was followed by another trip to Tayside and this time Larsson was on cue as the Bhoys defeated Dundee 2-1. Larsson was rested for the UEFA visit of minnows Cwmbran Town as the Celts won 4-0 for a 10-0 aggregate scoreline but he was back in action at the weekend when Hearts came to town, and he was on the scoreline yet again in the 4-0 victory. Further league points were racked up without the aid of Larsson goals when Kilmarnock (1-0) and Hibernian

(2-0) were seen off but sandwiched between those two away games was the home UEFA Cup tie against Hapoel Tel Aviv of Israel and the Swede hit both, one from the spot, in the 2-0 win. Following the Hibs win, Celtic were off to Israel for the UEFA away tie and Larsson was again on song with the only goal of the game for a 3-0 aggregate win. Back on the domestic front Aberdeen were put to the sword in a cut-throat 7-0 thrashing, with Larsson netting a hat-trick - but that would be the last of the goal action the Celtic Park crowd would see from their Swedish idol for quite some time. Celtic had been drawn against Olympique Lyonnais in the UEFA Cup and the first leg was to be played away from home.

Lyon were lying second in the French league so it was going to be a tough night for the Celts. Little did we know just how hard-hitting the game was going to prove for the Celts as, after just eleven minutes, the unselfish and hard-working Larsson exhibited one of the endearing aspects of his play - he was tracking back to help out the defensive midfield. And in an otherwise innocuous tussle with Serge Blanc, the Swede's studs caught in the turf and then came the moment that had everyone, not only Celtic supporters, cringing in horror. Larsson's lower leg was hanging at a seemingly impossible and sickening angle - instantly people feared for his career, surely not even a professional footballer could return from an injury like that.

Within seconds the club's doctor and physio, Roddy Macdonald and Brian Scott, were on the scene and it was clear to even those without any advanced medical knowledge that something was seriously wrong. Larsson was ferried straight away to Lyon's Eduard Herriot Hospital as the game carried on but few, especially those who were subject to repeat showings of the moment of impact on television, showed anything but the merest modicum of interest in the proceedings. Included in those viewers was Henrik's wife, Magdalena but despite the excruciating pain and all the obvious hullabaloo in the medical room of Lyon's Stade Gerland, the striker managed to put a mobile phone call through to his wife back home in Bothwell and assure her that he was okay. Henrik Larsson was probably the only person in the world who thought he was okay and while the rest of us wondered if he would ever play football again, at that moment he focused his thoughts with one aim in mind - the determination that he would again pull on the green and white of Celtic.

That was the beginning of a long process for Celtic's medical team in the rehab of Celtic's greatest asset and right from first diagnosis, club doctor Roddy Macdonald knew it would take time. He recalled: "From the pitch side I saw him going down, and it was clear we would be dealing with quite a significant injury. With an injury of that type, my immediate responsibility is to maintain a normal anatomical position and make sure the injury is stablised and not made any worse in moving Henrik from the pitch to the treatment area. Brian and myself were there with the help of the local stretcher-bearers, and as I recall it was a bit difficult communicating with them but I have to say they were very helpful. We immediately put Henrik in a fracture strap which immobilises the leg and maintains normal anatomy and removed him from the pitch on a stretcher, taking him inside to the treatment area. My immediate dilemma was that the game was continuing but obviously Henrik was seriously hurt and would need us to stay with him as some important decisions would have to be made at the hospital, the game only being eleven or twelve minutes old.

"As it happened, Jack Mulhearn the previous Club Doctor, was attending the game and I managed to contact him to come down pitch-side and take over medical cover for the game whilst I accompanied Henrik to hospital. Prior to going to hospital, as I recall, he was in so much pain he was given intravenous morphine and once completely stable we then organised transport to the hospital. I remember at the time pondering whether it would be feasible to get Henrik home that night to have him reviewed the following morning with an Orthopaedic Surgeon in Glasgow. The decision would have been taken out of our hands had the skin surface over the shin area been breached as this would have required immediate surgery. However, thankfully this was not the case.

"Following assessment by the French Orthopaedic Specialist in Lyon, we decided to place Henrik's leg in a support back slab which maintains normal anatomonical position. This back slab is a plaster which does not completely encompass the whole leg but holds and maintains normal position and caters for any excess swelling. We then agreed to get Henrik home on the charter flight that night and I administered pain relief as he needed it on the plane. We were then met by an ambulance at the other end and he was taken to Bon Secour hospital for the rest of the night. Having spoken to the local Orthopaedic Surgeon in Glasgow, Mr Bill Leach, it was decided that the best way to manage this kind of fracture would be to operate and stabilise the fracture with an intra-medullary nail, which is standard procedure for this kind of fracture. This was then carried out at the Western Infirmary. As it happened, the operation was quite straightforward and there were no obvious immediate post-op complications and, in fact, most of Henrik's rehabilitation went without any real major hiccups."

Although the injury was obviously very serious, it turns out that the images flashed up on television and in the papers were not quite as horrific as first thought. The doctor explained: "What you saw in all the photographs, in fact, was an exaggerated picture of the situation and what you were actually seeing was his shin-pad protruding at an angle because of the underlying fracture itself. I think that most people thought that this was actually his shinbone protruding when in fact it wasn't, but certainly it was quite a dramatic picture. What made this operation more interesting was the ability to return to football at an earlier stage than would have been seen possible. In previous years this injury would have been treated conservatively, with the leg being placed in a full length plaster and this could easily have meant the footballer being out for at least nine months of rehabilitation.

"That rehabilitation would be more arduous because of obvious muscle-wasting and joint stiffness. The intra-meduallary nailing procedure is really internal fixation of the fractured bone and allows the player to progress with walking and then more advanced rehab in a shorter time frame. The rehabilitation as well is, therefore, obviously more stimulating for the player."

It was then that the Celtic Medical Team kicked in, with the Doc and Physio Brian Scott overseeing the recovery progress. "Henrik's rehab was definitely a team effort. It could be described as multi-disciplinary," the doctor explained "Obviously, this started with the Orthopaedic specialist's input and then myself and Brian dealing with the day-to-day assessment and physical therapy side of it. We also had input from Kenny McMillan, our Exercise Physiologist, who put together some fitness and strength programmes for Henrik. Irene Riach was involved closely monitoring Henrik's diet and assessing him on a regular basis. Jim Henry, our Fitness Coach, was also involved in the later stages, so it was clearly a team effort. Again, as I recall we felt that realistically the season would be over for Henrik. This kind of injury can take anything for six to nine months rehabilitation to make a full recovery. As I have seen with other players, however, a good recovery would be closer to the six-month mark. One blip on Henrik's rehab was when he played in a reserve game and was tackled, with the result of a slight irritation over the fracture site. This set him back and at the time Henrik probably felt that the European Championships were out of the equation at that point as well. This settled down, however, and in fact he eventually played in the last game of the season against Dundee Utd which put his rehab period to just over six months."

Considering that many thought the injury was career-threatening at the outset, there was great surprise and joy when Henrik made it back before the end of the season, but Macdonald was not caught unawares by the early come-back. He said "As with any serious injury you're concerned with any post-operative complications which may hamper his rehabilitation, and in that sense there might be a concern of this being career-threatening but certainly this wasn't the case with Henrik. In fact, Orthopaedic Surgeons do carry this operation out quite routinely now but obviously the ability to play top class football raises the stakes more.

"This can be seen when footballers make recoveries from injuries that would, to a lay person, take twice, maybe even three times longer to recover from. It is almost certainly to do with their heightened powers of recovery relating to their fitness levels and obviously the intensity of the medical input they receive day to day. In retrospect, the time frame was realistic for Henrik and it was a real bonus for him to play in the European Championships. There is no doubt that his high fitness levels contributed to his ability to return so quickly with the Sweden squad at the European Championships. Even from a day-to-day point of view in training, it is easy to see how hard Henrik works and how high his fitness levels are."

While Roddy Macdonald, Brian Scott and co were overseeing and monitoring the return to fitness of Larsson, business as usual still had to be taken care of on the pitch but, try as they might, could it possibly be business as usual without the obvious goalscoring and general play-making attributes of the Swede? Celtic's league form at that time read: Played 8, Won 7, Drawn 0, Lost 1, Goals for 25, Goals against 3, Points 21. Very healthy indeed and at first the supporters were delighted with the input of the Dream Team but any team losing

Larsson would pay a heavy price and Celtic were no different. The post-Larsson period started well enough with a 2-1 away win over St Johnstone but that was followed with a 1-0 home defeat to Motherwell. There were plenty more victories to savour but these were interspersed with defeats and draws - and these were becoming more frequent as the season marched on. Mark Viduka, another Celtic hero in the making and another who was to have various problems with the hierarchy at Celtic Park, had to take over the mantle of principal striker while tutoring the apprenticeship of the up-and-coming Mark Burchill. In a bid to bolster the attack, the ageing youngster Ian Wright was signed from West Ham but the move proved to be short-lived, with the former England striker hitting three goals in nine appearances before moving on to Burnley. Viduka was still firing in the goals, aided and abetted by Burchill and Tommy Johnson, with Eyal Berkovic and Lubo Moravcik also keeping up the goal rate - but they couldn't compete with Larsson in the goalscoring stakes and Celtic in general, and John Barnes in particular, paid dearly.

Things came to a head on February 8, 2000 when lowly Inverness Caledonian Thistle visited Celtic Park on Scottish Cup duty and the Celts were simply expected to sidestep the former Highland League club and move on to the next round of the competition. It didn't quite turn out that way and one of the most embarrassing nights in Celtic's history was upon us. With Larsson sitting helpless in the stand, the demoralised Celtic team were taken to the cleaners by the First Division outfit. The Larssonless Celts lost 3-1 but it was the goings on off the park that would have the biggest impact on the not too distant future for the Celts. Amid a half-time dressing room bust up with Viduka refusing to return to the field of play, John Barnes lost any control he had over his charges and he was gone. Kenny Dalglish was in charge of the team from then on in but even his undoubted aura at Celtic Park had already been tarnished with the same brush and the writing was on the wall. Dalglish started well, with a 3-0 win over Dundee at Dens Park then a 1-0 defeat of Kilmarnock in the League Cup semi-final followed by another win over Dundee at Celtic Park, this time by a more convincing 6-2 scoreline. But March also featured a defeat at the hands of Hibernian, not to mention two reverses against old rivals Rangers including a 4-0 away defeat. Celtic did lift the League Cup by defeating Aberdeen 2-0 in the final at Hampden but that was scant reward for the pre-season expectations when the Dream Team arrived. The Celtic support only had one thing to look forward to and that was the return of the Magnificent 7 - but would that be before the end of the season?

Larsson had gone through the grueling process of rehabilitation and endured the setback of the injury in the reserve game against Hearts. The rehab started very, very simply; walking with both crutches, walking with one crutch, walking with no crutches. It was that basic to start with and those first wobbly steps were the first on the road back to pulling a green and white shirt over his head at Celtic Park. The process may sound basic but getting the legs moving again as early as possible was vital as muscle wastage sets in very quickly and no time was lost on eradicating that likelihood. Bike work was also an important aspect of the early procedure and soon Larsson was burning up just as much energy on the bike as he usually does during a match. The striker soon started running and although he personally felt he had hit a brick wall as the rehab process levelled off, by the time Celtic visited Portugal for the mid-winter break, he had started to tentatively kick a ball again, though not in the presence of reporters. Then came the short run in the reserves before it looked like disaster had struck again. After the Hearts second-string match, Larsson played down the injury but deep within himself he knew it was possibly a serious setback. Again there were sharp pains in his leg and he seriously thought it was broken again. Psychologically he was right back down there where he had started back in Lyon. He was limping badly and the wound was painful, but although the Celtic support would have been quite happy for the return of the Magnificent 7 at the start of the following season, Larsson had his heart set on playing for Sweden in that summer's European Championships.

Just when he was deliberating if it was all worth it or not, he decided to take a short break in Portugal with Marc Rieper who was commentating on the Portugal v Denmark friendly taking place that week. Three days of golf was just what the doctor ordered and it was on the flight back to Glasgow that he decided he would make one last concerted effort to make the Swedish squad - but that would obviously require playing club football first and he would have to convince Kenny Dalglish that he was not only ready and up for it but also that he would come through any game unscathed. In a meeting in Dalglish's office on the final Thursday of the season, the striker explained that he was feeling great. He was back to fitness and was dying to play. The final game of the season was against Dundee United at home and it would be his last chance to appeal to Swedish coach Lars Lagerback that he was ready and available for international selection. Dalglish was unmoved. He didn't want to take the chance on another setback and risk spending the summer months trying to get Larsson fit yet again.

The desperate Larsson pleaded his case again and Dalglish relented slightly. He would have to think about it though and promised the striker he would give him an answer the following day. On the Friday morning the nervous Larsson knew he still had to convince the manager but the Swede took to this particular training session as he had never done in any before, he had done all he could. His heart was pumping as he walked across the Barrowfield turf but Dalglish had seen enough, he called the Swede over and told him he could have 25 minutes the following day against the Tangerines.

Seven months after his Lyon nightmare, Larsson had finally earned a place on the bench and the massed Celtic support were overjoyed at seeing the Swede warm up before the game. By the second-half, the cries of 'We want Larsson, We want Larsson' had grown to a deafening crescendo and Dalglish could ignore them no more. To an ear-splitting wall of sound, Larsson stepped over the white line to replace Eyal Berkovic. The supporters who had arose in adulation at their returning hero had hardly sat back down in their seats before they were back off them - almost right away Larsson drove forward and fired in a low drive that rocketed past the post from all of 25 yards. Dundee United defender Tony Smith was the party pooper who spoiled the perfect comeback when he cleared another Larsson effort off the line. Celtic won 2-0 but, as in Lyon although for different reasons, no-one was bothering about the score - Larsson was back.

Chapter IV

The Return of the Magnificent Seven
Three cheers for Henrik - the Treble

ALTHOUGH the 1990s were done and dusted, it was odds on that Celtic would spend the first summer of the new Millennium conducting their by now annual search for a new manager. Nobody fell flat on their back when Kenny Dalglish and Celtic parted company after a season that started with so much promise and hope but simply fizzled out. It took off like an Exocet missile but finished with all the firepower of a cheap throwaway cigarette lighter in a gale force wind. The Celts had finished the campaign on the 69-point mark, an embarrassing 21 points behind Rangers, seven games worth of full points and, with both sides having drawn six games each, seven victories was exactly the difference between the teams. Three of those defeats were at the hands of the Ibrox side and the other Old Firm meeting was a 1-1 draw. Rangers scored 10 goals against the Celts, only conceding three. The mathematics dictate that just four one-goal victories over Rangers would have had the championship at Celtic Park but if only life were so simple. Playing an out of tune second fiddle to Rangers was bad enough but defeats against the likes of Dundee United, Hibernian, Hearts and Motherwell were the real psychological killer blows. Then there was the Inverness Caley debacle that made Celtic the laughing stock of Scottish football. There was the slight face-saver of lifting the League Cup but even this lightweight Celtic team were punching below their weight in this tournament.

They started by defeating lower-league Ayr United and the other three opposition teams - Dundee, Kilmarnock and Aberdeen - all finished in the bottom four of the Premier League. Celtic won that competition without conceding a single goal but, under the circumstances, this was nothing to make a song and dance about. Not that singing and dancing are par for the course at wakes in any case, but something had to be done to keep Rangers from conducting proceedings with the upper hand. Top of the list was the installation of a new manager but Celtic had not only burned their fingers but also caught them in the till in this scenario before. Practice makes perfect so they say but despite seven managers in the 1990s, not to mention three interim managers in the shape of Frank Connor, Billy Stark and the slightly more established

Kenny Dalglish, Celtic still weren't getting it right. Admittedly this was for many and varied reasons but all the excuses in the world were failing to appease the faithful supporters. Celtic had to get it right and get it right quickly. The supporters were sick of their club being the yearly summer joke as the managerial search was as much an annual source of football merriment as the now traditional Ne'erday screening of BBC Scotland's Only An Excuse. The right man had to be found. He needed to have managerial experience. He needed to have tasted managerial success. He needed to know what Celtic was all about. He needed to be a Celt ... Enter one Martin O'Neill.

If Wim Jansen abated the cold and unwelcome wind of European failure by signing Henrik Larsson from Feyenoord three years earlier, then the man who was to stifle the breeze was introduced to the supporters atop the five stairs leading up to the hallowed portals of Paradise on June 1, 2000. There was an entirely welcome and unexpected change this time. The announcement had been made early, the green and white scarves still bore the sweat and tearstains of the season just past such was the speed of the appointment. There was not the usual Limbo period through June and July. Supporters could enjoy their foreign holidays without the by now habitual practice of trying to read the back pages of the Scottish newspapers in some Mediterranean shop without forking out the couple of quid to actually buy them. There were to be other changes too - all for the better.

Irishman Martin Hugh Michael O'Neill stood in the seasonal rain of a Glaswegian June and paused until the cheers of the gathered throng had died down before thanking them for waiting in the inclement weather. He then uttered: "It's an absolute honour for me to be the manager here, I will do everything I possibly can to bring some success here to the football club."

Those words were to echo down the following seasons. The aside, "bring some success" is surely akin to Wim Jansen's "effective contribution to the team" quote about strengthening the team just days before he bought Larsson. And the phrase, "the football club" was one that was soon to become very familiar indeed. O'Neill fitted all the criteria concerning being the 'right man'. He had managerial experience. He had managerial success. He knew what Celtic were all about and he was a Celt. But there was one more basic but vitally important criterion - he had to be available, and like Feyenoord in the case of Larsson, O'Neill's former employers, Leicester City, weren't going to give up without a fight. That Martin O'Neill was now a Celt was never in any doubt but Leicester wanted financial recompense and they were going to make it very difficult for John Robertson and Steve Walford, vital elements of the O'Neill trinity, to follow their boss to the East End of Glasgow. The bureaucracy failed to stand in the way of all three teaming up, though, and the Celtic support could look ahead to the new season with renewed vigour.

Martin O'Neill was born in the Derry town of Kilrea on March 1, 1952 and soccer shared his spare time with Gaelic football in which he played for both St Columb's in Derry and Belfast's St Malachy's College, but it was when playing the association version of the game with Rosario Youth Club in Belfast that he caught the eye of Irish League club Distillery. After joining the football club in August 1969, it was in those austere surroundings that he first sampled the taste of European football when he managed to find the net against the mighty Barcelona in the Cup-Winners' Cup of season 1971/72.

His first European sortie was due to having helped Distillery defeat Derry City in the 1971 Irish Cup final. Scoring against Barcelona put him in the spotlight and in October 1971, after 49 appearances and 26 goals, he crossed the Irish Sea to sign for Nottingham Forest for £15,000. In 1977 Forest gained promotion to the top flight down south and they also won the Anglo-Scottish Cup. Amazingly, they won the title in their first season as well as beating Liverpool in the League Cup final, and then lifted the Charity Shield against Ipswich Town. The following season Forest beat Malmo 1-0 in the final of the European Cup in Munich, although O'Neill didn't play in that match, and also beat Southampton in the League Cup final. In 1980, Forest seemingly achieved the impossible when they lifted the European Cup for the second successive year and this time O'Neill was in the team that beat SV Hamburg 1-0 in Madrid thanks to a John Robertson goal. The same year they had beaten Barcelona in the European Super Cup and were runners-up in both the league and the League Cup, where they lost to Wolves. Just for good measure they also beat Nacional in the World Club Championship.

In 1981 Forest lost the European Super Cup to Valencia but, after 372 appearances and 60 goals, O'Neill was on his travels when Norwich City bought him for £250,000. While with the Canaries he helped them gain promotion to the top flight but before going on to captain Northern Ireland in the World Cup in Spain - the first Roman Catholic to skipper the Northern Ireland team - he was on the move again after just 11 appearances and one goal for Norwich. This time the asking fee was £275,000 and the destination was Maine Road but after only half a season with Manchester City and no goals in 16 appearances, he was on his way back to Carrow Road for £150,000 where he played a further 64 games and scored 12 goals for Norwich. In August 1983, Notts County snapped him up on a free transfer and he played 81 times and scored seven goals for his last club as a player. After 593 appearances and 106 goals throughout a professional career that witnessed its fair share of trophy success, it seemed that a career in managership was tailor-made for O'Neill and that's exactly what happened. He served his apprenticeship by starting at the very bottom and working his way up.

As Grantham's most infamous citizen, Margaret Hilda Thatcher, was beginning the downward spiral of her political career in 1987, Martin O'Neill chose the town to start the upward spiral of his managerial career when he took over Southern League - Midland Division Grantham Town. He managed the club for two years before leaving in 1989 for a short spell with the quaintly named Shepshed Charterhouse. The managerial call gripped O'Neill again in 1990 when he took over the reins at the Football Conference League's Wycombe Wanderers in July of that year. In 1991 they lifted the FA Trophy by beating Kidderminster in the Wembley final and the following year they won the Bob Lord Trophy, a cup contested by Conference clubs. In 1993 it was all happening for Wycombe and they needn't worry about entering for the Bob Lord Trophy again. O'Neill led the Wanderers to the Football League by wining the Conference and they also lifted the FA Trophy again by defeating Runcorn at Wembley. The amazing run continued when O'Neill took Wycombe from the Third Division to the Second Division at the first time of asking by beating Preston North End in the Wembley play-off in 1994.

His remarkable qualities had not gone unnoticed and in June 1995 he joined First Division Norwich City, but a few months later, in December, the call came from Leicester City. In his first season he steered the Filbert Street club to the Premiership by virtue of winning a Wembley play-off with Crystal Palace. The following season Leicester City lifted the League Cup by defeating Middlesbrough in the

Hillsborough final and the Foxes were in Europe for the first time since 1961. In 1999 they reached the League Cup final again, only to lose to Tottenham Hotspur, but the following year they lifted the trophy yet again by beating Tranmere Rovers at Wembley. It was little wonder that club directors throughout the country were sitting up and taking notice of this young manager and the men in suits at Celtic Park were no different.

So Martin O'Neill was in place to lead Celtic into the new-fangled Scottish Premier League with 12 teams now in the top set up, a winter break for most of January and a cut-off point to split the division into two halves - the haves and have nots for the final five games of the season. This meant they would play five teams four times while they played the other six only three times! The league campaign also started earliest this season, with no League Cup or qualifying European games against minnows to warm up with before the fight for vital championship points began. Celtic faced a tricky curtain raiser with their new manager in a trip to Tannadice to take on Dundee United. Mark Viduka was off to Leeds United before the new manager arrived.

The squad had been strengthened, though, with the acquisition of record Scottish signing Chris Sutton from Chelsea for £6million and Martin O'Neill had put his BBC punditry during that summer's European Championships to good use by enlisting the defensive qualities of Belgian Joos Valgaeren from Roda JC in Holland for £3.6million. But the big fear for the Celtic support was how would Henrik Larsson recover from his lengthy and costly break of the previous season? True, he had come though the Swedish stint in the European Championships unscathed but the rough and tumble of the Scottish Premier League was another thing altogether. How would he cope, both physically and mentally, with the more grueling aspects of the Scottish game and how was his psychological frame of mind?

Such was the esteem held within the Celtic support for Larsson that their worries were not of a selfish nature, they were specifically altruistic. They genuinely feared for Larsson the man, Larsson the Celt who was one of them, rather than fretting about the capacity of a striker who may or may not score pots of goals for them. Henrik's worries were their worries - but they needn't have worried in the least.

King Henry the Sixth, Part II (Act IV, Scene I)
"True nobility is exempt from fear."

Old Shakey got it right on the button again and the Celtic King Henke of the year 2000 could well have carried on with the rest of the line, "More can I bear than you dare execute." Yes, the new improved Henrik was back. Remixed, remastered and with the original artwork restored. The rehabilitation was such that a slight limp noticeable when he walked even before the injury had disappeared - a minor miracle of sorts, but can the divine intervene on behalf of the divine? He was back, firing full blast on all cylinders and sticking the most famous tongue in football out at all and sundry at every opportunity - and there were going to be plenty of them.

The dreadlocked deadlock was finally over and it took just 36 minutes of his first full game back in the Hoops for Larsson to answer all the questions asked of him and extinguish all the fears. In darting forward from midfield, Paul Lambert was brought down but referee Hugh Dallas played the advantage and Chris Sutton's attempt on goal was blocked by Jason De Vos. The ball fell to Larsson and nanoseconds later it was nestling in the back of the net following a 20-yard left-foot shot from the Swede. Larsson was back big style and it wasn't just his goal that was earning all the plaudits. After the game, Martin O'Neill said he had told his striker: "Before this match I thought you were a good player but I was wrong - you are a fantastic player!"

David McCracken pulled one back for the home side with a header but it looked like Celtic now had a 'Dream Team' on the park, with Larsson and Sutton spearheading an attack so sharp you could cut yourself just by looking at it. And it was the big Englishman who saved the day and wrapped up the crucial first three points in the championship battle by striking home the winner in the 67th minute. Larsson was back, Celtic were back and it was back to the drawing board for every other team in Scotland. In the previous two league curtain raisers, Celtic had triumphed 5-0 over both Dunfermline and Aberdeen respectively, but this seemingly tight scoreline was valued 10 times more than those 10 goals put together. The execution of the game with the return of Larsson, the knitting in of the new players and the accent of the new manager, not to mention his trackside antics meant so much more at the dawning of this new season. There was something in the air, something so corporeal you could almost touch it, never mind smell it.

The Bhoys returned to Celtic Park for the next league match when Motherwell, who had beaten Celtic twice and drew once the previous season, came visiting. This was the sort of match that would be the test for Larsson which most fans were dreading. It should have been played in bouts rather than halves with a 'seconds out' call and the clang of a bell rather than a whistle. Celtic's Chris Sutton and Jackie McNamara, along with Motherwell's John Davies, were red-carded but referee Alan Freeland should have been red-faced for each of those decisions. This was your archetypal physical battle and although Larsson was not to score he came through it intact while Stilian Petrov came up with the goods by netting the only goal of the game.

After the 1-0 league win, Martin O'Neill's first European jaunt with Celtic had a happy outcome and Larsson was on the scoresheet again in the Grand Duchy of Luxembourg with the Celts rattling four past Jeunesse Esch to no reply. Another home league encounter beckoned as Kilmarnock travelled up to Celtic Park and presented O'Neill with a new experience as Celtic manager - the opposition took the lead. When Andy McLaren scored in the 15th minute it was the first time the Celts had been behind in nearly five hours of football under O'Neill, but the Super Swede was to come to the rescue by netting the equaliser five minutes after the break. In the absence of the suspended Sutton, Tommy Johnson fired in the winner 23 minutes later and another three valuable points were in the bag.

Hearts were the next to feel the sharpness of the rapier-like Celtic cut-throat offensive when Sutton with two and Larsson with yet another goal put the Celts up 3-0 at Tynecastle by half-time. Hearts hit two in the second period but they sandwiched a Lubo Moravcik goal to give a 4-2 scoreline for the Bhoys and the 100 per cent record was maintained. Midweek welcomed European action again with the visit of Jeunesse and it was a fringe Celtic team minus the likes of Larsson and Sutton that triumphed 7-0 over the Duchy minnows for an 11-0 aggregate score. The resting of the key men wasn't purely in reaction to the healthy 4-0 first-leg lead over a 'lesser' team. It was proactive rather than reactive as the coming weekend was to witness the first Old Firm meeting of the season - Martin O'Neill's first clash with Dick Advocaat's Ibrox side and this was being billed as the first big test for the Irishman.

There were still those who doubted that Celtic could cut it on the big stage with Rangers and there were those who were openly willing the Bhoys to be knocked from their early-season pedestal. There were those who thought Celtic didn't have the guts to overcome Rangers or maintain this winning run for very much longer against any team. Martin Hugh Michael O'Neill thought differently though...

The Magnificent Seven, Sandinista! (Side I, Track I)
"You lot! What? Don't stop! Give it all you've got!"

Why keep getting all Shakespearian about it when you can bring in The Clash to give it a bit of good old welly? And that's exactly what Martin O'Neill's Celtic gave to Rangers on Sunday, August 27, 2000 - and plenty of it. The Celts certainly gave it all they got urged on by Martin O'Neill in a way that made Joe Strummer's antagonistic and belligerent rallying call seem tame by comparison, this was a Green and White Riot - and this lot didn't stop, not until the final whistle when the last goal went in. Celtic didn't just simply beat Rangers. They toyed with them. They teased them. They tore them to shreds. They tormented them and they showed them just exactly who was the Boss.

Oasis main man Noel Gallagher witnessed the action and he just couldn't believe what was going on all around him. He couldn't believe it before the game. He couldn't believe it at half-time and he certainly couldn't believe it at the final whistle. Oasis were in Glasgow to play at the Gig on the Green and as more than 50,000 Celtic fans belted out the band's hit 'Roll With It', the songwriter called his brother Liam on his mobile phone in amazement to let the lead singer know just exactly what he was missing - if Oasis played through a million-watt PA it could never have sounded like this - and the game hadn't even kicked off yet. By the end of the game you would have needed a chisel and extremely big hammer to knock the smile off his face.

But amid all the fanatical hysteria, a game did break out and it had barely kicked off when Alan Stubbs knocked Lubo Moravcik's corner into Larsson's path. The Swede's shot appeared to be going wide until Sutton read the situation beautifully and after only 43 seconds the Celts were in front. It was the fastest Old Firm goal in the Premier League since Danny Crainie fired home against Rangers, also in his Old Firm debut, on April 10, 1982. The Celts won that game 2-1 but they were to do a little bit better this time. After just seven minutes it was

2-0 when Stilian Petrov flung himself at another Moravcik cross and Celtic Park erupted once more. Only another six minutes had gone before Moravcik this time teed up Paul Lambert, who duly smashed in number three. Just 13 minutes on the clock and Celtic were 3-0 up. The much-maligned Bobby Petta was one of the main tormentors and such was his unadulterated and public persecution of Fernando Ricksen that the Rangers man was not only subdued but also subbed with little more than 20 minutes played.

Another interested spectator sitting close to Noel Gallagher in the centre stand was Dutch national boss Louis van Gaal, there to cast his eye over Ricksen for the Holland squad - Petta got a call-up instead. Claudio Reyna pulled one back for the visitors before half-time but that mattered little to the delirious green and white hordes. The goal action still hadn't stopped and it was that man Larsson who converted the next one and rumour has it that Bert Konterman is still twisting his neck looking around for Larsson to this day. Sutton chested Jonathan Gould's long clearance into the path of Larsson, he nutmegged Konterman, gracefully ghosted past the Rangers defender and then clipped an awe-inspiring chip over Stefan Klos for number four. Rangers pulled another back from the penalty spot but there was no fear of these rampant Celts being upstaged on this form and on the 63rd minute, Larsson headed his second and Celtic's fifth.

The goalmouth action still wasn't over and if Chris Sutton started his Old Firm debut by scoring with virtually his first kick of the ball, then he might as well round off the day by scoring with his last kick and that's exactly what he did in the 90th minute. The final scoreline was Celtic 6 Rangers 2 and those of us who thought we would have to wait another 30-odd years to witness something like the 5- 1 game certainly weren't cursing our lack of foresight.

After the demolition-job, an overwhelmed Noel Gallagher said: "I didn't know what to expect. When I said this was a dream I didn't think it would turn out like this. What a day off. I'm still trying to take it all in. There was TWICE the volume, TWICE the pace, TWICE the passion and everything is TWICE the size of anything down south. There is usually a 10 or 15-minute lull with no singing in England but the singing up here went on continuously for about two hours. When the crowd were singing 'Roll With It' it got me right in the heart. I'll have to get hold of a Celtic songbook to catch up on some of the other tunes, though. I was sort of half expecting, half hoping that Celtic would win 2-1 but this is unbelievable."

The contemplation of facing Celtic and losing a barrow-load of goals was something that many teams, and more to the point, their goalkeepers, were starting to seriously consider. And the main threat was obviously coming from the Swede, who had already ruffled the net six times and this was still only August. One keeper who was more often than not subject to a bout of blows from the Larsson cosh was Robert Douglas of Dundee. Tired of the bruises to his ego he was presented with the ideal solution. He had the opportunity of a damage limitation option when Martin O'Neill moved to sign him. Later that season he made his Celtic debut in November against St Johnstone. So no goalkeeper knows the potency of Larsson more than Douglas as he has experienced the highs and lows of playing with and against the Swede.

The big keeper said: "You knew, especially if you were coming to Celtic Park in the days when Dundee were just promoted, that you were going to struggle. And I think he scored about every time. He's a quality player, his movement, his turns, he's great in the air for the height of him, he's strong, he's got everything, he reads the game fantastically well. That was the thing at Dundee, we had just come up from the First Division and you were coming to Parkhead with the likes of Henrik and Mark Viduka - an awesome pair. In saying that, we didn't go through any specialised coaching or training in the week leading up to the game. You just used to hope for the best. There's not much you can do as Henrik was a world-class player and he still is.

"But at that time we always seemed to give a few penalties away and I never got near any of them. He always changed his execution. I think his finishing is second to none. It was the same with dead-ball situations, when Henrik was lining up to take a free-kick. I don't think it matters whether you have five or six men in the wall. I don't like to have too many in the wall but no matter what, nine time out of ten Henrik can get it up and over and frequently hits the target.

"Then there was the prospect of Henrik bearing down on you in a one-on-one situation. Some of his goals have been fantastic but it's not easy, put it that way. I think that's one of his strong points because he can dip the shoulder on you, because he can go round you, he's quite happy finishing before that because has can end the move with a chip, so he's got everything in that category and probably that's one of his strongest points. Defenders and keepers fear him so much and the reason for that is his all-round game, he's verging on perfection. He's obviously happy at Celtic and enjoying his time, he's enjoying his football and I think that's one of the reasons he has stayed as long as he has. He's got everything to his game. It's not just that he's got one strength, I don't see any weaknesses in Henrik's game, that's the amazing thing about him. The papers make a crisis out of it if he doesn't score for two games and that's a joke. But the next game he will go out and score three or four, but that's the way it goes. He's fantastic."

The Celtic Park crowd were by now getting increasingly familiar with a certain theme tune. The old tongue in cheek litmus test for pinpointing an intellectual was that if you played him a certain 1829 overture from Gioachino Rossini, he would think of William Tell rather than the Lone Ranger. Prior to the late 1990s, the theme tune from The Magnificent Seven simply conjured up one solitary and enduring image - the shaved head of Yul Bryner. But by the turn of the new Millennium, even before the first bar of Elmer Bernstein's eternal classic was over, only one immediate image sprang to mind - the dreadlocked head of Henrik Larsson. The 1960 film's tag line was 'They were seven but they fought like seven hundred.' Not dissimilar to the attitude displayed by Celtic's talismanic number seven on the field. And, Bernstein's score has been rated as 'one of the greatest theme tunes of the 20th Century'. Surely another parallel with the instrumental Larsson there then. But although Bernstein's inspirational and rousing melody delighted the massed green and white hordes when it belted out of the Celtic Park PA system every time Larsson banged another one in, it was not to everyone's liking.

"It bugged me," said Rab Douglas recalling the days when Bernstein's theme was as popular with him as a poke in the eye with a sharp stick. "The Henrik tune, that was it when I was with Dundee. It used to come on all the time and it used to really bug me. When playing Celtic, especially at Parkhead, teams like Dundee used to play deeper and deeper, giving Celtic more chances and Henrik used to give us a lot of problems at that point. I'm delighted when I hear that tune now right enough!"

Douglas added: "When I signed for Celtic I didn't think back then that at least I didn't have to face Larsson again. You don't think of it that way. It was just coming here and meeting the manager and knowing the squad by playing against them regularly. It was quite a settled squad. It was maybe a good idea thinking about Henrik that way, though. I mean, he battered in 53 goals in that season so maybe it was a good idea. There is also the consideration that lining up for Larsson free-kicks in training makes you a better keeper. If you want to play against the best you are as well practicing against the best.

"There was one game last season when we worked on free-kicks one day in training with Henrik and Thommo. We scored straight from a free-kick in the match the following day so it just shows - that's the bonuses. I've been sold a few right ones by him in training though in one-on-one situations. Frequently, it's normally once or twice a week, to be honest. I think that's one of the best aspects of his game - going around you. That's me playing against him in training, though. Knowing that he's up front in a real game gives me and the rest of team real confidence. It's fantastic.

"If you are under pressure you know he will keep the ball, he holds it, he'll win a corner or produce a couple of bits of magic and you are a goal back up. Those skills are the qualities of Henrik. This season's game against Hibs at Easter Road was a prime example. I thought he had a quiet first-half and in the second he was there to tap in the winner. That's Henrik through and through. His work-rate is phenomenal. You saw him going into midfield against Dundee when Didier was sent off, and for me he is the all-round player. What makes him such a great player is that I think he's happy; he has that will to win. If he has to go into midfield he's quite happy, he'll track back. If he loses the ball up front he's one of the first to defend and that's the sign of a great player.

"Obviously I wasn't here at the time when he broke his leg but I think it showed that the team really struggled then. When you think of what Celtic paid for Henrik, £650,000, in today's terms he would cost ridiculous money and you are always going to miss a player like that. All credit to him, he has come back and although he hurt his jaw as well, touch wood nothing like that happens again. But he just wanted to get back playing and he did. It takes a lot of character to come back from an injury like that. You will now see him steam into a tackle and again that doesn't bother him. I think probably the first tackle after that leg break was the big one, once he got that first tackle in he would be over it, and all credit to a guy who comes back from an injury like that. But if Celtic missed him then, I don't know how much we'll miss him when he does go for good. How do you replace a player of that value then compared to what they are paying nowadays? It's going to take a hell of a talent spotter to find somebody to replace him. You never know, he might sign an extension - I certainly hope so. Away from the pitch he's a mad keen golfer. That's his thing but he's quite a private person and he's quite entitled to be. I don't think, deep down, he really likes the limelight and he wants to keep the personal life to himself ."

An incredible season for Larsson could only mean one thing - an incredible season for Celtic. And later on that term, the Swede was to prove that if he fell from the Kingston Bridge into the Clyde he would have came out with a salmon in each pocket. The occasion was a day out golfing for the Celtic squad and Larsson's mastery of precision in putting the ball exactly where he wants it was transferred from the football pitch to the golf course - he hit a hole in one! Rab Douglas recalled: "I was a couple of holes back and the next thing was we all heard the cheering. Obviously it could only be Henrik, so that sort of summed it up. I was waiting for the Henrik tune to come up! "

Paul Lambert remembered: "I was a hole behind him when he hit the hole in one and I just heard a kind of cheer. Nobody really knew what had happened and then we found out. It was unbelievable; honestly, I can just see him with his tongue sticking out. The life for him in Scotland has been great, he's been great for Celtic, it's been a two-way thing for him here but he's done well." And Jackie McNamara recollected: "I was playing that day and I was a few holes behind him. But apparently he has having a bad game and that was the only thing he did right all day. It might have been the luckiest hole in one you've ever seen. It's just typical that if anyone were going to get a hole in one it would be Henrik. That might have been luck but his game on the pitch isn't, that's ability. He has just got better and better, not just with Celtic but with Sweden. He may have given up his international career with Sweden a bit too early. From a Celtic point of view I hope he isn't giving up here, because even just now he's phenomenal."

And phenomenal was exactly the superlative to describe the 6-2 annihilation of Rangers when Larsson and the Celts not only took the them to the cleaners but also hung them up to dry in the wind of change blowing in from the East End of Glasgow. There was, however, the possibility of the familiar hangover following the party. Celtic supporters had grown used to seeing their heroes letting the haloes slip immediately after earning them. Winning the big battle but losing the war because of fatalities in lesser conflicts had for far too long been the downfall of Celtic's championship aspirations. Just ask Tommy Burns who out-pointed Rangers in 1994/95's Old Firm skirmishes but floundered in the league due to an abnormal run of drawn games against other teams. Far too many times had the victory dances been scuppered by the carpet being pulled from under us. This Celtic side, however, were not prepared to fly over Beecher's Brook only to trip over themselves on the flat. The League Cup was next on the agenda and with Larsson rested, the Celts helped themselves to a 4-0 win over Raith Rovers, with new singing Alan Thompson getting off to a flier. Martin O'Neill's third new Bhoy, signed for £2.75million from Aston Villa calmly back-heeled in Celtic's fourth of the night.

Long before Thompson's cheeky calling card nestled in the net though, the thoughts of many in the crowd would have been turning towards the weekend and the visit of Hibernian. Amazingly, despite the Celts' 100 per cent start to the campaign and hammering Rangers 6-2, it was not the Parkhead side who topped the league. That distinction fell at the feet of Hibs who, just one season after returning from the First Division, replaced their Edinburgh counterparts Hearts, as the main rival to Old Firm domination of the league. At 3pm on Saturday, September 9, the Edinburgh greens took to the field at Celtic Park as table-toppers, 17 minutes later their jacket was on a shaky nail as Larsson converted a penalty, by 3.45pm said nail was decidedly shoogly when the magical Swede struck again and by the 90th minute it was ripped completely out of the wall by the claw-hammer of a Mark Burchill goal. This was no mean feat for the Celts as the Easter Road side reached the top by virtue of losing only one solitary goal in their previous six Premier League games. And it was Larsson who inspired the reverberating 'We Shall Not Be Moved' chorus emanating from the Celtic Park stands as the faithful hailed quadrupling the Hibees' goals against tally and the outright No.1 position at the top of the league. Rangers drawing 1-1 at Dundee may also have kept the refrain going as the partying crowd snaked their way through the streets of the East End after the game. One of the key elements in Hibs attaining top spot didn't take to the field against Celtic, though, and Didier Agathe was soon to swap the green and white of Hibs for the green and white of Celtic.

HJK Helsinki were circled as the next date in Celtic's diary, with the Finnish side visiting Celtic Park in the UEFA Cup first round proper and, again, it was Larsson on the warpath. The Swede reached double figures by netting a double for the rather pleasing tally of 10 goals in 10 games. Celtic were on their travels again for a Monday night game in Dunfermline and for a while it looked like Martin O'Neill's 100 per cent record was about to be relinquished until, you've guessed it, Larsson came up with the goods. Stevie Crawford put the home side ahead just before the hour mark but within a minute, Larsson levelled from the spot after Paul Lambert had been dumped in the box by former Ranger Ian Ferguson. Larsson not only scored the winner but he also played no mean part in creating it when he back-heeled the ball to Alan Thompson. The Geordie glided past another former Ranger in Barry Nicholson and returned the ball to the Swede. Larsson coolly rounded the keeper and stuck the ball in the net to score his ninth goal in just five consecutive games. Dundee were next on the horizon and although Larsson was off target this time, Stan Petrov provided the necessary goal for a 1-0 scoreline and O'Neill's 12th consecutive victory.

That 12 didn't become 13 didn't mean all that much in the big picture but it was a nail-biting cliffhanger as Helsinki's Paolos Rohia overturned Celtic's two-goal advantage from the Euro first leg to take the tie to extra time. However, two minutes into the second period of extra-time, Chris Sutton hit his sixth goal of the season to carry Celtic through to the next round. The 100 per cent domestic record was to fall also the following Sunday at Pittodrie as the 10-man Celts came from a goal behind to earn a 1-1 draw. And it was Larsson who ensured the Celts were at least unbeaten on the domestic front when he headed in just 10 minutes from time. But the head that rose to turn that ball in was distinctly different to the one which Celtic fans had paid homage to by buying Henrik masks in their thousands. The dreadlocks were gone.

They had been shorn off in a moment of spontaneity. Just two days before the Aberdeen match he was on his way home when he turned right to the hairdressers rather than left to his house. He had worn the dreadlocks since he was 16-years-old and had toyed with cutting them off before his injury but he obviously had other things on his mind then. But on that day after training the willpower took over and he went from clipping the ball over keepers to clipping his trademark locks from his head. The obvious Biblical Samson parallels were there - would Celtic's goalscoring Samson lose his strength after being Delilahed?

Henrik Larsson without his dreadlocks was like - well, Bob Marley without his dreadlocks. On a counterpart with Larsson replacing Yul Bryner as the image of The Magnificent Seven theme, anytime a Rasta walked down the street people would point out the bloke with the 'Henrik haircut' rather than the Bob Marley dreads. But the Celtic marketing squad put a brave, as well as a new, face on things and produced a new range of Henrik masks, still with the protruding tongue but with the newly modelled shaven head. Mercifully, the dreads weren't Henrik's only trademark - that was goals, and plenty of them. The Samson quips were just so Old Testament. The New Testament was in its Genesis and the Gospel according to Henrik was let there be goals - so be it.

Newly promoted St Mirren were the next team to try blunting the Larsson/Sutton spearhead but they failed, not miserably, but they failed nonetheless. The big Englishman gave Celtic a first-half lead but it wasn't until the 86th minute of the game that Larsson presented one of his informative and enjoyable classes on the art of taking free-kicks. A cross into the box seemed the only logical option and with over 60,000 in the stadium, every single one of them was expecting just that - except one - and it wasn't Derek Scringmour in the visitors' goal. Larsson took the difficult option and made it look easy by curling a vicious low drive into the far corner - 2-0 and another three points were added to the tally.

McDiarmid Park was the next destination on a rain-sodden night when even the ducks were scuttling indoors while muttering profanities about the Scottish weather. Celtic kicked off in the shallow end and deepened their resolve for the title with a well-earned 2-0 victory, with Joos Valgaeren getting his name on the scoresheet for the first time. Valgaeren was joined on that sheet by the more familiar Larsson. The Swede netted a second-half spot kick to keep up his healthy goals bank balance with another deposit and Celtic were five points ahead at the top. That rounded off the first leg of the league campaign. Celtic had played all 11 other teams and had remained unbeaten. Only Aberdeen blemished an otherwise spotless complexion with that 1-1 draw at Pittodrie and Celtic had taken 31 points from a possible 33. They had scored 26 goals while the miserly defence let in only eight and kept five clean sheets. Larsson had netted 12 of those 26 goals and the Swede seemed in no mood to slow down.

The second phase of the campaign started like the first, with a 2-1 over Dundee United and Larsson getting the first goal but this time the other counter came from Alan Thompson. The date of United's visit to Celtic Park was October 21 - the first anniversary of Larsson's horrific injury in Lyon. Rewinding to that fateful night and the dreadful image flashed across the television screen, few would have thought that, a year to the day later, Larsson would not only be scoring never mind playing, but that his goal would help keep Celtic in front at the top of the table AND a massive 12 points in front of Rangers.

Larsson had truly exorcised the ghosts of doubt and a few days later he would make a return trip to France to play Bordeaux in the UEFA Cup. Larsson had a much happier journey this time and when Christophe Dugarry put the home side in the lead, it was Larsson who equalised just two minutes later from the spot after he was tripped by Lassina Diabate. Three days later the Celts were back in action and although Larsson failed to find the net, the goals still flowed - for both sides unfortunately. Celtic drew for the second time that season in a fluctuating 3-3 draw with Motherwell at Fir Park. But how referee Hugh Dallas or his linesman failed to see that Johan Mjallby's second-half effort was clearly over the line was beyond everybody - and the TV cameras. The League Cup beckoned again and yet once more a shadow team minus the likes of Larsson took to the field despite the more than worthy opposition of Hearts at Tynecastle.

That was the night when the 'C'mon the Hoops' chant was adapted to 'C'mon the weans' as the young guns displayed their firepower. Youngsters Stephen Crainey and Jamie Smith scored as the 90 minutes finished 2-2. Another from the reserve ranks in the shape of Colin Healy gave Celtic the lead before the not so youthful Lubo Moravcik and Jackie McNamara really tied things up for a 5-2 scoreline. That was the Celts though to the semi-final but there would be a three-month wait before that game - against Rangers.

Back on the league front, Celtic weren't monopolising the good news market in the headlines. Kilmarnock were on a 12-game unbeaten run. The Ayrshire side had put in a remarkable stint since Celtic defeated them 2-1 back on August 13. Celtic emerged from Rugby Park victorious and despite many scoring opportunities it was only a 60th minute Alan Thompson goal that separated the teams at the end of the 90 minutes. All attention turned to Europe once more and the imminent visit of Bordeaux for the UEFA Cup second leg and hopes were high after Larsson's vital away goal in the first leg. Expectations were thrust even higher when Lubo Moravcik fired Celtic into the lead in the second-half but Celtic were just 11 minutes away from reaching the third round for the first time in 17 years when Lilian Laslandes struck to take the game to extra-time. And right at the death, in injury time to be precise, Laslandes struck again to kill off Celtic's European hopes for season 2000/01.

Celtic rose from the Euro disappointment in fine style with an electric performance against St Johnstone, Larsson netting twice in a 4-1 league victory at Celtic Park as Robert Douglas made his debut in goal. The Bhoys were to take their tally to 10 in two games with the visit of Hearts the following week. Larsson hit another two in the 6-1 victory over the Edinburgh side as the Celts revved up for the next Old Firm meeting. With the 6-2 game still fresh in the memory, hopes were high. But although the Swede got in on the act with another goal, it was a day he, his team-mates and the Celtic support would rather forget as the Ibrox side gained revenge. The 5-1 defeat was embarrassing but ultimately not demoralising or psychologically damaging to Celtic's drive to the title. That was followed by a 0-0 draw with the other title challengers the following week, Hibs. But even missing out on five points in two consecutive games merely dented their campaign hopes.

Celtic got back on the winning track with the visit of Dunfermline but only after an early shock when Jason Dair opened the scoring for the Pars in only 50 seconds. Moravcik equalised then Larsson was at his cheekiest when he nutmegged the keeper to put Celtic in the lead and Tommy Johnson sealed the points in a 3-1 win 10 minutes from the end. An enthralling game followed at Dens Park when a last-gasp winner from Didier Agathe in a 2-1 win kept the three-pointers coming in. And no-one celebrated Didier's final touch more than new Bhoy Neil Lennon, who made his debut that night after joining from Leicester City.

Another debut Bhoy burst on to the scene in the next match when Aberdeen came calling and paid the price for having the temerity to be the first team to dent Celtic's push to the title. The new Bhoy was Ramon Vega, who joined on a short-term contract from Tottenham

Hotspur and he stated his intentions straight away by scoring twice. Larsson was not to be upstaged, though, and he thumped in his first hat-trick of the season with Jamie Smith adding another for a 6-0 victory. Celtic's first and only visit of the season to Love Street was next up and after Agathe had put Celtic ahead in the first half, Larsson sealed the points. The Swede kept up his incredible goalscoring record in the next game as the Celts triumphed 4-0 over Dundee United at Tannadice. Larsson's 23rd minute spot kick was his 96th goal in Celtic's colours. So, with the 100th on the horizon and the visit of Rangers just three games away... well what could be nicer?

The Larsson philosophy, however, does not make room for such niceties and if he were four short of the magical century milestone then he would get that out of the road as soon as possible. And in just 33 short minutes of the second half against Kilmarnock at Celtic Park on the first day of the year 2001 he did just that. With Celtic already ahead through Chris Sutton, Larsson hit in the 53rd, 70th, 73rd, and 86th minutes to reach the historic landmark. Celtic actually scored five goals in that 33-minute period with Sutton claiming his second in the 6-0 win.

With the first-footing of Kilmarnock safely out of the road, the winter break kicked in and Celtic jetted off to Florida for a well-earned break in the sun. But to acclimatise themselves to the rather more chilly weather of a British January they kicked off with a friendly on their return. Norwich City physio, Tim Sheppard, was the recipient of the testimonial at Carrow Road and 6,000 Celtic fans made the trip down on an absolutely freezing cold night. The home side took the lead in the first half and doubled their advantage nine minutes after the break, but it was Larsson who pulled one back two minutes later with a truly exquisite left foot hooked volley from the corner of the box. The Celts went on to win 4-2 and returned north in fine fettle to restart the campaign.

Stranraer was the first port of call in Martin O'Neill's opening Scottish Cup tie and, with the Inverness Caley fiasco of a year earlier still fresh in the memory, the game was deemed exciting enough to be televised live. No such shock this time, though, as the Celts won 4-1. Larsson wasn't to be seen on the scoresheet that night but it would be the only Scottish Cup game that season in which he didn't find the net. League football returned with a trip to Tynecastle to face Hearts and Larsson carried on from where he left off against Kilmarnock. It was

2001: a race odyssey in the goalscoring stakes as far as the Swede was concerned and he opened the scoring in the third minute with a header - the first of another hat-trick. This teed up Larsson and Celtic for a crucial double header against our oldest rivals.

The first was the midweek League Cup semi-final at Hampden Park and as far as Old Firm games go this was nothing to write home about - apart from a penalty for each team, a glut of fiery exchanges between the players, 11 yellow cards, four red cards, two Rangers fans staging an invasion of the pitch, and a 3-1 win for Celtic to put them into the final - just the sort of outcome the Glasgow constabulary loves. The win, with Larsson finding the net twice yet again, also meant that Celtic were the only team with a realistic chance of lifting the Treble. Sutton volleyed Celtic into the lead as early as the sixth minute and 10 minutes later Larsson repeated his sublime lob from the 6-2 game and again he all but crafted the goal himself. He robbed Rangers defender Bob Malcolm of the ball before heading goalward and lobbing Stefan Klos to put Celtic 2-0 ahead.

Then came the first of two soft penalties and the controversial decision sparked the first flurry of ugly activity - Rangers scored. Tempers flared again before the break. Caudio Reyna was booked for a 43rd minute tackle on Paul Lambert, two minutes later he committed the same offence on the same player but with no card produced this time. Reyna then bent over to let go with an outburst of insults at the grounded Lambert - still no further punishment. The second-half was no vicar's tea party either. Another contretemps between Johan Mjallby and Tore Andre Flo sparked heated outbursts from the dugouts but that was after Larsson had put the Celts further ahead after being brought down by Scott Wilson - again the penalty award could be deemed in the soft variety. There were only two minutes left on the clock when the game collapsed into the realms of stupidity. In two separate incidents, Rangers fans tried to invade the park, then the red mist seemed to come down over Reyna's eyes, literally. He brought down Bobby Petta, a scuffle ensued and Reyna walked, as did his team-mate Michael Mols and Celt Lubo Moravcik. Not content with the yellow and red cards he received on the pitch, Reyna contrived to earn another red after the game. This was Celtic's first League Cup victory over Rangers in 19 years and it set them up nicely for the Premier clash four days later.

Even the authorities seemed to know that this game wouldn't

erupt like the midweek clash as the police weren't armed when Celtic and Rangers lined up at Celtic Park on Sunday, February 11, 2001. Fernando Ricksen did get an early Valentine's card of the red variety, but compared to earlier events this match was tame in Old Firm terms. Celtic were already ahead when Ricksen walked just seconds before half time. Alan Thompson was the hero in the 16th minute and it was Larsson who provided the perfect flick through to the Englishman, who took the ball beyond Klos and into the net. From then on in Celtic weathered the storm, including a real one, which had the more pessimistic among us fearing that the game would be called off.

The 1-0 result put Celtic firmly in the driving seat, again 12 points ahead of Rangers and 11 ahead of second-placed Hibernian. There was talk of Martin O'Neill being awarded an OBE, the acronym being Over Before Easter. Celtic would have to wait to see in they could increase or maintain their impressive advantage as Scottish Cup duty was next in line with a trip to East End Park, but Dunfermline were to prove to be no easy slouches. All the goal action came late and started with that man Larsson who glanced home a delightful Thompson free kick in the 67th minute. The home side equalised through Andreas Skerla. Celtic took the lead again in the 87th minute and Larsson's goal was nothing but sheer class. He dummied Neil Lennon's pass and shimmied to accept Chris Sutton's lay off before clipping the ball over the keeper.

A replay was on the cards because a last-minute shot from Barry Nicholson deflected its way into the Celtic net and the Bhoys' cup run hit a slight bump. Another three points were picked up in the next league meeting as Motherwell visited Celtic Park, with 35-year-old Slovak Lubo Moravcik notching the solitary goal with a truly amazing free kick seven minutes from the end. Celtic's home league record under Martin O'Neill at that point read; Played 14, Won 14, Drawn 0, Lost 0, Goals for 44, Goals against 7.

The Irishman had a 100 per cent home record and Larsson had scored 17 of those goals in front of the delirious Parkhead faithful. But the record was to falter slightly, although not drastically, when Hibernian came to Celtic Park on February 25. A Swede still got on the scoresheet but this time in was Larsson's international partner Johan Mjallby who put Celtic ahead in the 22nd minute. Celtic's 100 per cent home record was still on until five minutes from the end when Frenchman Marc Libbra equalised.

Next up was a double header against Dunfermline, the first game away in the league and the second at home in the Scottish Cup replay. Larsson was to be on target in both games to maintain his astonishing record. His strike in the league encounter at East End Park was sandwiched by a Stan Petrov curler and Irishman Neil Lennon's debut goal for the club. In the midweek game Celtic strolled into the quarter finals of the country's oldest competition with a 4-1 win over the Fife club. Ramon Vega paved the way with the first two goals and Larsson was twice upended in the box and on each occasion he converted from the spot. Thanks to having to squeeze the replay in, Celtic's next game just days later was the quarter-final and Hearts visited Glasgow to try and stop Celtic's surge towards the treble. It was Larsson again with the vital goal when he headed Celtic in front from an Alan Thompson cross and the Bhoys were in the semi-finals where they would meet Dundee United. Celtic's next opponents were St Johnstone at McDiarmid Park and what should have been an evening of celebration was soured by the news that Stilian Petrov had broken his leg in a challenge seven minutes from time.

Tommy Johnson, from a sublime Larsson pass, gave the Celts the lead in the first half only for Stewart McCluskey to equalise for the home side. Larsson sealed the points with yet another header from yet another Thompson cross. Rangers had lost 2-0 to Dundee at Ibrox, meaning the Celts had now opened up the chasm of a 16-point gap at the top of the table. Any talk of the championship was put to one side, though, as the League Cup final intervened and one third of a possible historic Treble took precedence.

Celtic hadn't successfully defended the League Cup trophy since season 1969/70 but, on paper at least, this was their best chance of doing so in a long time. Kilmarnock supplied the opposition and the Celts had come out on top in their three league meetings so far that season - 2-1, 1-0 and 6-0. However, the Celts weren't exactly expecting a cakewalk. The Ayrshire side were battling it out with Hearts all season at the top of the chasing pack behind the title-chasing trio of Celtic, Hibernian and Rangers. And they had defeated Hibs 2-0 in the quarter-finals, although they had lost out to the Edinburgh club at the same stage of the Scottish Cup.

They were determined to lift a trophy but they had the misfortune to come up against a Celtic team who were determined to lift all THREE trophies - and they also had the misfortune to come up against an on-fire Henrik Larsson. The game remained in deadlock at the break but just three minutes after the break the Celts were one small step nearer the Treble when Larsson fired in an acrobatic volley past Gordon Marshall in the Killie goal. Just before the hour mark Kilmarnock were handed a lifeline when Dallas sent off Chris Sutton for a clumsy rather than cynical foul but the harshness of the decision inspired the Celts. Yet another Larsson goal followed in the 74th minute but it was the third and final goal of his cup final hat-trick that was the highlight of the day out on the South Side. Again he made this one himself and finished by dragging the ball round Marshall with the studs of his boot before slotting home. It was sheer genius - nothing less. One down, two to go - the Treble was still on.

The following weekend had Celtic scheduled to travel to Pittodrie on the Sunday while Rangers entertained Dundee United at Ibrox 24 hours earlier. Another possible run of the mill weekend at the top of the table was turned on it head when the Tangerines (United that is) triumphed 2-0. Instantaneously, the fact dawned on us all that Celtic could be champions by the following Saturday. The league could be over before the SPL's innovative league split. The wheat would be separated from the chaff before the wheat was separated from the chaff as it where. Aberdeen away (Sunday), Dundee home (Wednesday) and St Mirren home (Saturday) were all that stood between Celtic and the championship. None of the games were classics. Neither were they pretty. Larsson didn't score a goal and there were no resounding victories ... but none of that mattered.

A scrappy April Fools Day game at Pittodrie was sealed by a 72nd goal from Didier Agathe when he hit the ball on the turn and it went through Jamie McAllister's legs and past Ryan Esson in the home goal - 180 minutes to go on the championship clock.

Dundee trooped down to Celtic Park knowing they could only delay the inevitable and they almost succeeded. It was Larsson who set up Johnson for the opener when the Geordie side-footed the ball under Jamie Langfield in the fifth minute. The nerves were settled. Or so it seemed until the 67th minute when Juan Sara met a lob from Giorgi Nemsadze to slot home from close range past Rab Douglas. The nerves went from settled to shattered in that instant and it looked like the big Saturday night out may have to be shelved. Or at least that was the case until six minutes from the end when Johan Mjallby scored a goal that could hardly be classed in the Pele department - but nonetheless he would have difficulty in repeating the importance of the strike. An Alan Thompson corner deflected, bounced and bobbled about the Dundee penalty box before Mjallby somehow scrambled it home. It seemed to take an eternity to cross the line. But cross the line it did - 90 minutes to go on the championship clock

And so it was Saturday. Not any old Saturday but Saturday, April 7, 2001. True, Celtic had six games left with which to win only three points to claim the championship, but why wait? Why not do it at home when there were only another two homes games penciled in? Why not do it today when there were 60,440 fervent fans urging you on? Why wait indeed? As it turned out this was not a day for the feint-hearted, another five games to go or not. Stage fright may have been the order of the day but surely we could do it against the bottom-of-the-table relegation-bound Paisley team. Just as he did a few days earlier, Larsson set up Tommy Johnson for the deadlock-breaking and all-important goal. This goal, however, was from the Pele department - Mrs. Pele that is. The Geordie seemed to hesitate, go off balance and fluff his shot but somehow it trickled past Ludovic Roy and over the line - 53 minutes to go on the championship clock

Celtic peppered the St Mirren goal time after time and on a couple of occasions Larsson came close to doubling Celtic's lead and securing the championship then and there. But on the few occasions St Mirren ventured forward, over 120,000 hands were raised to heads in fear of the Paisley side equalising. Then it happened, the ref blew the final whistle and we all named that tune in one, 'Championees, Championees' - 0 minutes to go on the championship clock, it had run out of tock but there was still plenty of 'Tic left. Two down, one to go - the treble was definitely still on.

Bedlam broke out in the Celtic Park stands as Martin O'Neill and his team took the first of many bows in front of their adoring fans. The championship trophy had yet to be presented, there were still five league games still to play, there was still a Scottish Cup semi-final to be negotiated but the main job had been taken care of. And Celtic would have a bite at the Champions League cherry the following season. In just 33 games Martin O'Neill had transformed a squad of 20-odd players and fulfilled the dreams of countless thousands throughout the world. He had not only turned the club on its head but also fortified the faithful through his own faith and the conviction that he would simply try his best as the words "I will do everything I possibly can to bring some success here to the football club" clearly testify. Doing everything he possibly could did not involve taking his foot off the accelerator at this crucial stage in the season. There was still the matter of the Scottish Cup and there were records still in sight, both for the club and for Henrik Larsson.

Dundee United would be no pushovers in the semi-final, however. The Tannadice club had disposed of Rangers by 1-0 in the quarter-finals and they were more than keen to make up for a disappointing league campaign. Larsson kept up his love affair with Scottish Cup goals by diving at the near post to meet a Chris Sutton cross in the 31st minute to put Celtic in front. Then in the 78th minute he cemented Celtic's bid for the final when he converted from the spot after he had been upended by Danny Griffin. A Larsson pass then laid on the third for Jackie McNamara and the Celts were in the final despite a consolation goal from Derek Lilley five minutes from the end. The Swede had taken his personal tally for the season to 49 and in doing so had surpassed the post-war scoring record of Charlie Nicholas, who banged in 48 goals in season 1982/83.

The following Sunday was prize-giving day and although Celtic had won many championships, this was the first time the brand spanking new SPL trophy had been adorned with green and white ribbons. But there was the small detail of a game to be taken care of first, with Hearts there hoping to be the party poopers who would burst all the balloons. Lubo Moravcik appeared from the bench in the 63rd minute and almost immediately set the pulses racing with a 20-yard shot that Niemi just tipped over, but it's our party and we'll sigh if we want to. However, just a few minutes later the little Slovak accepted a pass from Larsson before slotting the ball home for the icebreaker. After that there was no need to play spin the bottle as the party was in full swing and no-one was heading off to the kitchen for a bit of peace and quiet, they all wanted to be in the big room where all the action was.

The final score was 1-0 and now the party could really begin with the presentations of the trophy amid a sea of green and white tickertape. As the two-tone April shower cascaded down to the hallowed turf, green and white balloons floated up in the opposite direction to hover over the East End sky and as they dispersed in all directions, Martin O'Neill told the crowd, "We'll try and have three things for you to celebrate."

There were still four league games to be taken care of before any thoughts of that final celebration and there were one or two landmarks still to be considered. At that point Celtic had scored 82 league goals and although it was a long shot, it was still feasible that they could creep up to the 100 mark. What was entirely more possible, though, was reaching the 100-point mark. The Celts sat on 91 points and they had four games with which to win those nine points. The drawback was that the first two games were away to Rangers and Hibernian, the teams that had put in the most concerted challenge to Celtic all season. There was also the slight shortcoming in that Celtic hadn't beaten Rangers at Ibrox in seven years, but then plenty of other taboos had been laid to rest that season.

So, on April 29, the first half finished goal-less before two wonderfully sublime peaches from Moravcik had Celtic fans dancing in the aisles of Ibrox. But then came the crème de la crème and for once Larsson wasn't using his tongue in celebration of a goal. At Ibrox, against Rangers, just four minutes from the end, Henrik Larsson stood in front of the Broomloan Road stand with the five digits of his right hand pointing to the heavens while the thumb and forefinger of his left hand met in a circle. It was the BIG FIVE ZERO.

Larsson had scored his 50th goal of the season and he couldn't have picked a better place to do it. And the goal couldn't have been any sweeter or from a tighter angle. The final score was 3-0 and Larsson had fired in his sixth goal past Rangers that season. Next up was the trip to Easter Road for a Scottish Cup final dress rehearsal and Larsson was in a 51st state of euphoria as he bagged another goal in Celtic's 5-2 victory over the Hibees. That took his league tally for the season to 35 goals, equalling Brian McClair's 1986/97 post-war best for Celtic. In fact, Larsson had equalled the best since season 1935/36 when the amazing Jimmy McGrory banged in an unassailable 50 league goals.

That was the two most difficult games out of the road but as fate would have it, Celtic took nothing from their final two league games. After only one defeat all season, they lost the two end-of-season meaningless games. After scoring in every single game except the 0-0 draw with Hibs, they failed to find the net in the final two matches. And after an unbeaten home run under Martin O'Neill, they lost that when Dundee won 2-0. In fact that was Celtic's first domestic defeat at Celtic Park since March 8 of the previous season when they lost 1-0 to Rangers. The final league game was a 1-0 defeat at Rugby Park and Celtic stopped on the 97-point mark, just one game away from the magical century. Players had been rested and even Larsson missed out on the opportunity to surpass McClair's record as he was wrapped in cotton wool for the big one - the Scottish Cup final and the last portion of the three-leaf clover that was the Treble.

The Treble yell went up before the game and the Treble songs were blaring out after it. It was the Battle of the Greens at Hampden Park and the final score was Celtic 3 Hibernian 0. Jackie McNamara replaced the injured Lubo Moravcik after only 18 minutes and little more than 20 minutes later he had fired Celtic into the lead. Didier Agathe rolled the ball in front of the sub and he strode into the box before firing a left-foot shot past Irishman Nick Colgan into the net. The game was still on a knife-edge, however, until three minutes after the break when McNamara found Larsson and the Swede buried a left-foot shot into the top corner of the net for his 52nd of the season.

Number 53 wasn't far away and 10 minutes from the end, Gary Smith pulled down the newly-crowned King of Kings and the referee pointed to the spot. Larsson gave Colgan no chance with the spot-kick and that was that. The Treble was in Celtic's hands for only the third time ever and for the first time since season 1968/69. As a benchmark to illustrate how difficult it is to win a Treble you only have to look back the glory days of Jock Stein's nine-in-a-row years. For each of those nine seasons, apart from 1967/68 when Dunfermline hit Celtic with an early Scottish Cup exit, the Celts were on the brink of a Treble.

In every other season they had won the championship AND reached the final of BOTH national cups. Despite being within touching distance of the treble EIGHT times they only won it twice. So this was a truly glorious season for Celtic and all the more remarkable since it was Martin O'Neill's first in charge. The game is all about scoring goals at one end while stopping them at the other, and the Celts scored 138 goals while conceding only 42 and keeping 25 clean sheets. And it was Larsson who netted an amazing 53 of those goals, the same tally that Jimmy McGrory reached in season 1927/28. And just four less than

McGrory scored in season 1926/27 when he rattled in 57. Little wonder then that Larsson picked up the Scottish Football Writers' Association Player of the Year award to add to the one he won two years earlier. He also snapped up the Scottish Professional Footballers' Association Player of the Year award, again he had won this two years earlier.

But the personal pinnacle was surely the European Golden Shoe for being the top scorer in Europe. Larsson however, is a team player and these personal awards would have meant nothing to him if Celtic had been pipped at the post in each of the competitions. Second prizes are for losers and Larsson is a winner in every sense of the word. Goals are just the means to an end and if that means laying off the ball to someone else, that's exactly what he does. He is as much a goal maker as a goal taker and his input to the glorious Treble season of 2000/01 is impossible to assess just by dissecting mere statistics alone. But to put it simply, "He made us happy when skies were grey."

Chapter V
It Was Twenty Years Ago Today
Back-to-Back championships

THE wind of change that was sweeping through Celtic Football Club had blown the club to new heights under the managership of Martin O'Neill, and the Golden Shoe of Henrik Larsson had gone a long way to taking them there. The Celts had not only won the league but they had also turned a 21-point deficit from the previous season into an amazing 15-point surplus over the course of one season. Martin O'Neill had also steered the Celts to both Scottish Cup and League Cup triumphs at the first time of asking, so everyone knew it would be more than difficult to emulate the successes of the previous term. Added to that there was the prospect of Celtic entering the realms of the Champions League, which was daunting to say the least.

In their previous attempt after Larsson's first spectacular season at Celtic Park when the 10 was stopped, the Bhoys never went further than the qualifying stages, St Patrick's Athletic were sidestepped but Croatia Zagreb put paid to any hopes of the group stages and the UEFA Cup beckoned. Our stay there was also a short one, with Vitoria Guimaraes dealt with before FC Zurich provided a not too unexpected slap on the face. Season 1999/2000 handed us UEFA Cup entry and Cwmbran Town and Hapoel Tel Aviv were taken care of, only for Olympique Lyonnais to take care of us in the third round. The UEFA Cup was also the door to Europe for Martin O'Neill's first season in charge, with Jeunesse Esch and HJK Helsinki taking early exits at our expense before another French side in the shape of Bordeaux dealt with any possible threat from Celtic. That was the trouble with European football, any time we came against a team of any substance we struggled and for far too long that had been Celtic's story in European football.

Of course, there may have been a few hard luck stories along the way such as in Larsson's very first season under Wim Jansen, when Inter CableTel and Tirol Innsbruck fell to the Celtic goal machine before Liverpool progressed in the UEFA Cup thanks to the away goals rule. But Celtic's European ills started a long time before that and you would have to go back to season 1979/80 to find a run of any excitement on the continent. That was the last time Celtic had been involved in

European football beyond Christmas but what exactly does that turn-of-the-year hurdle really mean in any case? In that season's European Cup, Celtic put out Partizan Tirana and Irish side Dundalk before being edged out by Real Madrid in the quarter-finals in March. The European Cup back then wasn't all that different to our League Cup exploits now - you play a couple of games and you are in the final. In 1979/80, Celtic only played two teams and they were through to play in Spain beyond Christmas, the next time Celtic would play in Spain beyond the New Year would require beating a lot more than two teams - and they wouldn't be Partizan Tirana and Dundalk.

In 1998/99, Celtic played four teams in Europe and were out by the start of November so European football was changing on and off the field and Celtic had to adapt. The first season Martin O'Neill took Celtic into Europe as Champions they were to play a total of five teams and still be out before Christmas but there was no doubt that massive strides had been taken and that the Celts were desperately unlucky to exit that season - when Celtic won the European Cup in 1967 they only played five teams and had passed the Christmas milestone by only beating two of them. In season 1998/99 they had already met two teams and the league campaign had hardly kicked in. However, at this early stage in Martin O'Neill's managerial reign at Celtic, any strides forward in European football were always going to be looked upon as a bonus.

And when Celtic were drawn out of the Champions League qualifying hat with Ajax of Amsterdam it looked like that benefit could very well be short-lived once more as the Dutch club could hardly be described as anything like the minnows Celtic usually met at the first European hurdle - that it didn't turn out that way was as spectacular as it was mildly surprising. Celtic supporters were to witness more European glamour in the autumn and winter of the year 2001 than they had in nearly 30 years and it simply whetted the appetite for more.

The European bonus was definitely the cream on the cake. The ingredients to bake that cake were mixed in the blender of domestic football and the more bread and butter games of Scottish football were the true qualifying rounds for further the European glory. The big question was, though, was the glorious championship win of season 2000/01 a flash in the pan or could Celtic win two successive titles for the first time in 20 years since the legendary Billy McNeill kept Celtic at the top in seasons 1980/81 and 1981/82? If the truth were known, Celtic came teasingly close to clocking up five consecutive titles in a row during that period. In season 1978/79 the Celts in Billy McNeill's first season in charge hoisted the league flag high. The following season they finished just one vital point behind Alex Ferguson's Aberdeen. Then came Celtic's run of two consecutive titles and the season following they were again just one point behind Jim McLean's Dundee United.

That's all rhetoric, however. The fact was that the hungry Celtic support had been starved of consecutive titles ever since but they sensed that something was in the air. Martin O'Neill had an aura around him. Henrik Larsson had an aura around him. And, increasingly, it seemed that this team were displaying the characteristics of natural born champions with a natural born predator up front in the shape of the super Swede. And the striker was quick to let his intentions be known, even in the pre-season games where he started off as he had finished the previous season by rippling the back of the net.

After the pre-season jaunt, London club Queen's Park Rangers were first to feel the sharp end of Larsson's tongue when it took him only two minutes to get right back into the swing of things. He latched on to an Alan Thompson through ball and slotted it over the keeper for the first goal in Celtic's 2-0 win. Celtic returned north only to face another London club when former Celt John Collins' Fulham visited Celtic Park for a friendly. Celtic emerged to a resounding heroes' reception in their first home game since the lifting of the Treble and the newly promoted Premiership club played their part in the party proceedings. They unfurled a giant banner proclaiming "Congratulations Celtic on your Treble-winning season. Good luck in Europe'. Touching as it was, Celtic were in no mood to return the good luck message and Larsson in particular was a thorn in the side of the Cottagers. He struck twice, the first arrived when he rose high to convert a looping cross from Bobby Petta in the 29th minute. Then 14 minutes after the break he slotted home again after good work by Didier Agathe and Chris Sutton. Young striker Shaun Maloney, who had made his debut when Larsson hit his golden 50th of the previous season against Rangers, added a third four minutes from the end for a 3-0 win.

All in all, it was a good Friday night for the Celts as the occasion also saw the unveiling of Martin O'Neill's latest signing, Bobo Balde who was introduced to the crowd at half-time. The massive Guinean defender was signed from French side Toulouse and was the newest cog in the well-oiled machine that O'Neill was constructing. Over the course of O'Neill's tenure thus far there were to be many and varied changes in the look and strength of the Celtic squad. The first season had seen the introduction of Chris Sutton, Robert Douglas, Didier Agathe, Neil Lennon and Alan Thompson, while the likes of Vidar Riseth had gone to 1860 Munich and Alan Stubbs to boyhood heroes Everton. There had also been the temporary but successful term of Ramon Vega, but when it came to signing a longer term deal, the big Swiss player was apparently talking telephone numbers so he was given one - the number of the nearest taxi firm. As well as Bobo Balde, other players to come in during the second season would be John Hartson from Coventry, Momo Sylla from St Johnstone and Steve Guppy from Leicester City.

The squad was gelling together nicely but it was pretty much a typical line-up for Celtic's next pre-season game, the visit of Premiership side Sunderland. One big talking point, though, was the battle of the Golden Shoe winners. The current holder, our own Henrik Larsson was coming head-to-head with previous winner Kevin Phillips and although the match could never be described as a classic, the Swede's firepower came out on top against the English side. The final score was 1-0 with Celtic's 68th minute goal coming from a Larsson penalty after Bobby Petta was downed in the box.

Celtic's next action was of the competitive variety as we were back in the nitty gritty of SPL action, defending the Championship won so convincingly the previous season. St Johnstone were the visitors for the curtain raiser with nigh on 60,000 inside Celtic Park and an international TV audience watching live as the Celts vied to keep their hands on the SPL trophy for the second successive year. But first there was the opportunity to salute the efforts of season 2000/01 when chairman Brian Quinn hoisted the championship flag - the real reward for the season. For while the gleaming trophy may be wrapped in green and white ribbons, it spends most of the season encased in glass deep within the bowels of Paradise, with only those who take tours of the park able to snatch a glimpse of the domestic Holy Grail. Whereas, the championship flag flies above the North Stand at every home game for all and sundry to see - including the visiting teams. Once the flag was unfurled the champions emerged from the tunnel and the capture of the first three points of the season was top of the agenda.

It was clear that the Perth side weren't there to simply make up the numbers and they were going all out to spoil the party atmosphere with the main tormentor for Sandy Clarke's men being one Momo Sylla - Martin O'Neill was to ensure that the Ivory Coast player would not be causing Celtic problems again that season. Celtic triumphed by 3-0 and each of the goals were to come from unlikely sources. Johan Mjallby set the ball rolling in the 36th minute when he glanced home a header from a Bobby Petta cross. Then Paul Lambert, who had only scored one of Celtic's 138 goals the previous season, had a rush of blood to the head and converted two within nine minutes. The first came from a cheeky one-two with Didier Agathe while the second was a wonderful left-foot volley. There were no points at stake in the next game, just the reputation of Celtic, the Old Firm and Scottish football as the argument raged at the time as to the validity of the big two from Glasgow joining the Premiership down south.

Not just the legality or ethics of the situation but to whether or not they could actually cut the mustard against the cream of English football. To be fair, Celtic had only lost once to an English club since Martin O'Neill's arrival - against Manchester United in Tom Boyd's Testimonial - but the obvious retort was that friendlies don't count in the big picture. The great Jock Stein, however, always maintained that Celtic don't play friendlies. And the outlook of the club was that any 'friendly' match whether it be a testimonial match or not, was always viewed as a Challenge Match no matter what the circumstances. It was also pointed out that Celtic's most recent run of matches against clubs from across the border were, with no disrespect to QPR, Fulham and Sunderland, hardly meetings with the crème de la crème of England's finest.

Celtic's next match was a return fixture against Manchester United - at Old Trafford. The occasion this time was Ryan Giggs' Testimonial and this was an unofficial Battle of the British champions. A 'friendly' it may have been, but try telling that to two teams who were intent on proving that they were the best in Britain. Try telling that to Neil Lennon who was brutally scythed down by Paul Scholes. Try telling that to David Beckham who received a slap in the face by Chris Sutton and try telling that to the 20,000 Celtic fans who took over Manchester city centre before enveloping Old Trafford in a sea of green and white. Celtic fans react to testimonials like no other group of supporters and that is one of the reasons why the club are invited to take part in so many. The other being that the opposition know at least they will get a game of it.

And with so many supporters turning Old Trafford into a mini Celtic Park there was renewed calls from Bhoys' fans to make this a more regular occurrence by joining the Premiership. It was a fantastic day out and they wanted more of it. The truth is though, if Celtic were playing Man United on a regular basis in the Premiership we would be more likely to receive 2,000 tickets rather than the 10 times we had for the Giggs Testimonial. In any case, after Celtic's performance in the Theatre of Dreams, it was highly unlikely that Man U would be casting a vote in Celtic's favour if the case ever arose - Celtic ripped them apart and just kept on tearing into them. The game was only four minutes old and the Bhoys were already two up before Dmitri Kharine in the Celtic goal had even touched the ball. Chris Sutton and Neil Lennon were the scorers and although Ruud van Nistelrooy brought United back into it in the 24th minute, Paul Lambert restored Celtic's two-goal advantage five minutes later. Juan Veron pulled another one back 20 minutes after the break but Celtic hit back with an amazing free kick from Lubo Moravcik, which flew past Fabien Barthez in the home goal. Dutch superstar van Nistelrooy pulled another one back six minutes before the end but the game finished 4-3 in Celtic's favour and the big Scottish question was not going to go away.

The only disappointment on the night was that Henrik Larsson didn't score to help abate the old argument that he couldn't do in England what he regularly did in Scotland. The Swede would just have to wait to see if Celtic would be drawn against English opposition in Europe - it wouldn't be all that long of a wait. But Larsson's job was to score in competitive games and on return from Old Trafford that's exactly what he did on the Saturday at Kilmarnock with the only goal of the game, his first of the season and his 122nd in Celtic's colours. The game also saw the introduction of John Hartson for his debut from the subs' bench, to the delight of the travelling support. The Welshman had previously nearly signed for Rangers and the mood among the support was especially buoyant, as the Ibrox side had slipped up against SPL newcomers Livingston earlier in the day. If Celtic found it tough to break down Kilmarnock then surely they were awaiting a baptism of fire in their Champions League qualifying match against Ajax in the overpowering Amsterdam ArenA. To use one of Larsson's favourite Glaswegian phrases, the match, however, was 'Nae borra' and the awe-inspiring Celts played havoc with the Dutch side's home advantage by running over them 3-1, with the goals coming from Bobby Petta, Didier Agathe and Chris Sutton.

There was no Euro hangover when the Celts returned from Holland as Hearts came along the M8 to Celtic Park and went back home a few hours later with the vision of Larsson's tongue imbedded in their minds and The Magnificent Seven theme ringing in their ears. He struck just before the break, then nearly burst the net with another in the second half to earn a 2-0 win and another three points for the Celts. A week later it was Celtic's turn to travel along the M8, but before getting to Edinburgh they took the unfamiliar cut-off at Livingston for their first league game at Almondvale.

The newly-promoted club were to become the Hibernian of season 2001/02 and they proved that being a thorn in the side of Rangers a couple of weeks earlier was no fluke. They earned a 0-0 draw as Larsson failed to convert a penalty and Celtic's 100 per cent record was gone. Come midweek, Celtic suffered a rare home defeat, against Ajax, but at the end of the day it mattered little - Celtic were in the Champions League proper for the first time ever. Celtic went down to a solitary Wamberto goal but thanks to their heroics in Amsterdam went through 3-2 on aggregate. Martin O'Neill had made the Champions League dream become a reality and the rampant Celts celebrated in fine style by going on a fantastic 14-game winning run in the SPL and scoring 35 goals for the loss of only seven, with Larsson netting nine of the Celtic goals.

That run took them though to the verge of Christmas and started with a 4-1 win over Hibernian at Easter Road. A Paul Fenwick goal four minutes from the end was the first scored by a Scottish club against Celtic that season and one of only 18 they were to lose in the whole league campaign. Not that the goal made any difference to the outcome of the game as, when Larsson headed in an Alan Thompson corner on 30 minutes played, that was Celtic's fourth of the afternoon. That was followed by a 3-1 home win over Dunfermline, then Larsson hit the first two at Dens Park in a 4-0 win over Dundee. Aberdeen were next on the receiving end, when Larsson again found the net in a 2-0 win at Celtic Park.

It was that time of the season again, though, and a trip to Ibrox was the cards. In the greater scheme of things, the Old Firm meeting is the one game when the form card really flies out the window and this one was going to provide all the traditional talking points - red cards, booking etc. However, it had been a long and dreary 18 years since Celtic last came away with back-to-back wins over Rangers at Ibrox and although the end-of-season 3-0 win there was only four months prior to this latest meeting, it may as well have been a million years ago in Old Firm terms. However, no-one told that to the Celts, and when Larsson tapped a free kick to Stilian Petrov, the young Bulgarian fired in a rasper of a shot that eluded Stefan Klos to put Celtic one up. In the second period, Lorenzo Amoruso felled Larsson in the box and took an early bath for his misdemeanor. Klos palmed away the Swede's spot kick but Alan Thompson was to put the game beyond Rangers with a wonder goal, gliding through a trio of challenges before knocking the ball beyond the reach of Klos.

It truly was a superb goal and the match finished 2-0. Celtic had not only laid the 18-year hoodoo to rest but they also opened up a seven-point gap at the top of the table by the end of September. Fir Park was the next destination and Celtic had Henrik Larsson to thank once again for sealing up all three points. Lubo Moravcik opened the scoring in the 14th minute with a stunning 25-yard free kick, only for Greg Strong to equalise with just less than 20 minutes to go. The stalemate remained until just two minutes from the final whistle when Shaun Maloney was tripped in the penalty box. The Larsson eye-to-foot co-ordination was pinpoint sure this time and the 2-1 win maintained the seven-point gap at the table top.

Dundee United were next up at Celtic Park and the scoresheet for the 5-1 win had a fresh look about it. Shaun Maloney got the fifth for his second top-team goal, the first arrived in the earlier 4-0 win over Dundee at Dens Park. Bobo Balde scored his first Celtic goal in the 5-1 trouncing but John Hartson really burst on to the scene with a hat-trick.

The Welsh striker knew he would have a hard time breaking in to the team as the Larsson/Sutton partnership was always going to be a tough nut to crack. He said: "I knew about Henrik and obviously Chris as well, having played against him down south on numerous occasions.

The year I arrived Celtic had just won the treble so I knew it was going to be difficult. But the manager assured me that if I was playing well and was doing the things he knew I could, I'd be in the side. And it wasn't so much a case of taking his place or anything like that. It was more to get in and play with him. Obviously we found that system in Europe where Chris can play in the hole and I think the three of us have done very well together.

"If you look at our goals per games ratio, the teams we've defeated and the way we've played it's pretty good. But any time you go to a club there's always competition so I knew that was going to be the case. But Henrik's simply a fantastic all-round player. As a player, what's good about Henrik is that he's never happy to rest on his laurels. He always wants to do better and during games, if he's got a goal or two goals, he wants to then go on and get three or four. He's never satisfied with what he's done. You see him now, even at 32, he says he's going at the end of the season; he's adamant he's going so he wants to make sure he goes with a bang. He wants to do really well and he's definitely up there.

"I've been lucky, I've played with Ian Rush, Ian Wright, even in my younger days people like Kerry Dixon and people like that at Luton who were heroes of mine. Then there was Mark Hughes and now obviously with the Welsh team we've got Ryan Giggs and Craig Bellamy but Henrik's definitely up there with the best. And what's good as well is that he's done it in Europe, there are people who knock the Scottish League week-in-week-out saying that it's easier than down south. But I think he's more than proved himself to people with what he's achieved. Just look as what he's done on the international scene with Sweden, not to mention all the goals he has scored for Celtic against the top European teams."

Hartson added: "I'm not sure really sure what sets him apart from other players, probably his natural instinct, his eye for goal. There have been several games while I've been here and they've looked as if they were just fizzling out to a o-o or 1-1 draw. But then Henrik's just produced that little bit of magic. He seems to keep doing it time after time. We've all had our little bits of magic, including myself in the past when you can create something out of nothing - a great goal or whatever but the good thing with Henrik that sets him apart is that he seems to keep doing it all the time. That's obviously what the great strikers do and that's why they are so few and far between. But what probably sets him apart is his work-rate as well, which is immense, he works ever so hard and I don't think people realise how much he puts into training as well as his input on the park. And I think he's improved over the years at holding the ball up and his positional play.

"It's not just his natural goalscoring ability that sets him apart. He's very good to play alongside as well because I was actually surprised when I first played at how much of a talker he is. He talks a lot on the pitch and he helps you, he wants you to do well and another good attribute of his is that he's very, very unselfish. If he feels you are in a better position he will give you the ball. He's very much a team player, which you don't usually see with players like him who have got 200 and odd goals. We don't really socialise with each other outside of football, we train together we have a laugh and a chat but I wouldn't say we are best mates. He's a very private person which is fine, that's absolutely fine so probably the best understanding we get out of each other and when we get to know each other is on a Saturday. That comes when we play together for those 90 minutes. It's when we celebrate goals and good passes and touches together that it all comes together and that's great."

Hartson's rise to the top with Celtic has run in tandem with the re-emergence of the Welsh national team and the striker has been a major part in the recent glory run for his homeland. But Larsson's recent retirement from the international stage with Sweden has given Hartson food for thought although he is no doubt that the Swede could definitely carry on at that level if he wished.

He said: "Well I don't know if he's given up too early or not. I think it's something which obviously I'll think about in a year or two down the line. But it does benefit you playing just club football, and I think Henrik is really satisfied with what he's done for Sweden. He couldn't give any more, he's played in a couple of World Cups, European Championships, he's got 60 or 70 caps so only he knows. He's very much his own person but he can definitely go on at the highest level for a good few more years yet. He's still fit enough and looks strong. I don't know how he feels himself because who am I to tell him what to do. The same as I wouldn't have anybody telling me what to do. He's his own person but the one thing I would say is that he could definitely carry on at the highest level, I really believe that because he's still one of the best out there."

So Hartson was now on the goals trail along with Larsson, Sutton and the young Maloney but Celtic's next goal to seal three points in their long winning run was to come from a defender. Following the 5-1 demolition job on Dundee United, Kilmarnock were the next visitors to Celtic Park and, like the earlier trip to Rugby Park, a tight 1-0 outcome was the order of the day - and it came right at the death. The visiting Killie side certainly made life difficult for the table-toppers who took to the field without the talismanic Larsson. And stalemate ensued until injury time when a Stilian Petrov cross from a free-kick was touched on by Johan Mjallby to Joos Valgaeren who scrambled the ball into the net. It was a cliffhanger all the way but still the seven-point gap remained at the top of the table.

The next game produced an equally nail-biting climax with the second successive late, late show from the Celts when they visited St Johnstone's McDiarmid Park. The home side's Darren Dods gave Celtic the lead when he converted an own goal. The sinner became a Saint yet once more though when he atoned for his mistake by equalising to bring St Johnstone right back into the thick of the action just eight minutes later. With the Saints back on level pegging they really took the game to Celtic. But that man Larsson came to the rescue deep into injury time when he looped a superb free-kick over the wall and into the net - the run was still on. From there came an uncharacteristically tough encounter when Celtic travelled to Tynecastle. Celtic had scored 12 times on their previous three visits to the capital and Hearts had yet to win a single point in their seven prior attempts against Martin O'Neill's Celtic.

This meeting was to prove a great deal more difficult, though. The deadlock wasn't broken until four minutes before half-time when a crude tackle on Didier Agathe by Andy Webster saw referee Mike McCurry have no hesitation in pointing to the spot. Larsson's aim was true and another three valuable points were in the bag. That set Celtic up nicely for the following weekend's Old Firm clash when Rangers would come calling to Celtic Park.

Celtic went into this match knowing they could increase the gap to 10 points but were equally aware that a slip could mean Rangers narrowing the lead to just four points. Joos Valgaeren opened the scoring just three minutes before the hour mark when a Petrov cross from a free kick was knocked down by Bobo Balde and the Belgian was there to smash the ball in past Klos. Just 12 minutes later, a Neil Lennon through ball was played right to Larsson and as he was about to fire in, Bert Konterman pulled him down. The Swede simply picked himself up, dusted himself down and slotted home the spot kick. Rangers pulled one back in the 78th minute through Lovenkrands but the valiant Celts were to hold on for Martin O'Neill's fifth successive victory over Rangers and the 10-point gap at the top of the league was a reality.

Hibernian were the next visitors to Celtic Park and two first-half goals from John Hartson were added to in the second half by a magnificent, not to mention rare, goal by Neil Lennon for a 3-0 victory. Dunfermline were next as Celtic travelled to East End Park and another double from Hartson was complimented by counters from Bobo Balde and Alan Thompson in the 4-0 win. All three main strikers got their names on the scoresheet when Dundee came to Celtic Park the following weekend and lost 3-1. Larsson's counter was sandwiched by others from Chris Sutton and John Hartson for Celtic's 14th league win in a row. During the same period, Celtic also triumphed in two League Cup games, taking that domestic tally to 16 games as they scored 10 goals to no reply in those two games.

Lowly Stirling Albion were first up on November 6 and the Celts won 8-0, with Shaun Maloney taking all the plaudits with four of the goals while Hartson (2), Olivier Tebily and Colin Healy grabbed the others. SPL side Livingston provided a sterner test but Balde and Hartson gave Celtic a 2-0 win over the Almondvale side. The run had to stop somewhere, though, and so it did on January 22 at Pittodrie. In a bad tempered match, Aberdeen won 2-0 - a second-half penalty and a last-minute goal from a short pass back while Celtic were pressing to equalise. The match was Aberdeen's ninth consecutive home victory that season, the first time they had managed that since season 1983/84 and it was manager Ebbe Skovdahl's first victory over Celtic. Aberdeen were also the first Scottish team to score two goals against Celtic that season. The Celts could be forgiven for showing signs of tiredness however. Prior to their trip to Pittodrie their domestic record read: Played 20, Won 19, Drawn 1, Lost 0, Goals for 54, Goals against 7. An amazing set of statistics in their own right but all that was achieved while also taking part in a strength-sapping European run that gave the Bhoys real belief in what they could go on to achieve on the continent.

After their magnificent disposal of Ajax in the qualifying round,

Celtic were drawn in Group E with FC Porto of Portugal, Rosenborg of Norway and the Italian giants Juventus. Celtic's debut in the Group Stage was scheduled to be a home match against the Norwegian champions but the terrible events of September 11 in New York brought that midweek football to a close and the Celts were then flung in at the deep end with an away trip to tackle the mighty Juventus. Celtic were more than holding their own in the Stadio Delle Alpi when, just two minutes before the break, a Stilian Petrov shot was charged down and Juve broke forward, with Salas taking the ball to the right and creating space behind Joos Valgaeren before cutting the ball low into the box. David Trezeguet had the simplest of tasks in knocking the ball in from two yards. The Turin side went further ahead 10 minutes after the break Again, it was Trezeguet, this time a header from a Del Piero cross and the Celts looked up against it but with Larsson leading the line they refused to crumble.

In the 67th minute, the super Swede tapped a free kick to Petrov and his shot found the net with the aid of a deflection. The Celts flung everything forward and, after an earlier penalty claim, justice was finally seen to be done when Chris Sutton was bundled in the box by Birindelli. The King of Kings strode forward to calmly slot the ball low to Buffon's right. The large and noisy travelling Celtic support erupted but as the game fizzled to a finish, the strangest of strange penalty decisions foiled the great work of the battling Celts. Nicola Amoruso quite blatantly took a dive in the vicinity of Valgaeren. German referee Hellmut Krug pointed to the spot and Amoruso had the cheek to convert the penalty. Martin O'Neill was so incensed at the decision he was sent to the stand for the remaining seconds.

As a consequence of that he was also in the stand for the next Champions League game when Porto came to Celtic Park on Tuesday, September 25 and this time a Henrik Larsson goal gave the Bhoys their first three points of the Euro campaign. Didier Agathe won a corner on the right and Bobby Petta swung it over for Joos Valgaeren to provide a knockdown to Henrik, and the Swede poked it home. Larsson's goal earned the three points that saw the Bhoys leapfrog Porto and move into second place in the league table. By the end of the following game, Celtic amazingly topped Group E and the players and supporters were left to wonder how much stronger would their position have been had the referee been on the boil in Turin.

An Alan Thompson free-kick after Stilian Petrov was brought down in the 19th minute provided the only goal of the game against Rosenborg but Celtic's next two games were to be away from home. The first of these was against Porto in the Estadio das Antas and the Celts were given a football lesson from the Portuguese side. It could all have been so different if Clayton hadn't scored as early as the first minute but as soon as Porto had the upper hand they were going to use it to beat Celtic back down. Things didn't get any better in the next away match in Trondheim's Lerkendal Stadion against Rosenborg. And to make matters worse, former Celt Harald Brattbakk was the man who did the damage with two first-half goals. The situation left six-point Celtic having to beat Juventus and hope that four-point Rosenborg would beat seven-point Porto, if that were the case then the Bhoys would progress to the next phase of the Champions League.

Hoping for a Norwegian win, though, was a double-edged sword because if Celtic failed to beat Juventus then Celtic would sit at the bottom of the table with no European football to look forward to. On a magical night, however, Celtic did beat Juventus for one of their greatest European triumphs and Larsson converted another penalty in the amazing 4-3 win but Rosenborg failed to shock Porto and the Bhoys now moved in to the UEFA Cup.

The draw could have been kinder, though, but after their Juventus battles, the newly invigorated Celts had nothing to fear from Valencia and even a 1-0 defeat in the Campo de Mestalle didn't seem unassailable. And Larsson was the man who brought Celtic right back into the picture just before the break when he speedily latched on to a pass from Joos Valgaeren and curled the ball into the corner of the net. Celtic Park erupted in homage to the Swede as the Bhoys piled on the pressure but the game went into extra-time. Valencia survived the closest of close shaves when Pellegrino cleared a Larsson attempt off the line. The game went to penalties and Celtic lost 5-4 to end the European dream for another season.

Back on the domestic front, the Aberdeen defeat did little to halt Celtic's drive towards their second successive title as their taste for Champions League football had been well and truly whetted and they wanted to book their place for the following season. They went on another winning run in the SPL, with only draws interrupting their progress on the road to the flag flying once more over Celtic Park. And the name of Henrik Larsson was to crop up more often than not on the scoresheet. Following the defeat at Pittodrie, the Celts got back into the swing of things right away, with Larsson hitting a double in a 3-2 home win over Livingston on Boxing Day and the team finished of the year 2001 with Larsson again finding the net in a 4-0 win over Dundee United at Tannadice. Larsson saw in the New Year with another strike in a 2-0 home win over Motherwell, then a Celtic shadow side defeated Alloa Athletic 5-0 in the third round of the Scottish Cup. Back on SPL duty there was a 2-0 away win against Kilmarnock and then St Johnstone fell 2-1 at Celtic Park with Larsson scoring the first and when Hearts arrived the following weekend a Larsson double saw them lose 2-0.

The Swede was again on target in the next two games. The first was a 2-0 Scottish Cup win over Kilmarnock at Rugby Park, then it was off to Livingston for 3-1 SPL win. Celtic had John Hartson to thank for winning a point in the next game, a 1-1 draw with Hibernian at Easter Road but the league game following that was nowhere near as tight as Larsson was back on the hat-trick trail when he banged in three in a 5-0 home rout of Dunfermline. That set the Swede up for another personal milestone. When the Celts visited Dens Park and recorded a 3-0 victory over Dundee, Larsson's goal was his 150th in Celtic colours.

However, in the midweek leading up to Larsson's hat-trick against Dunfermline, Celtic relinquished their hold on the League Cup when they lost 2-1 to arch rivals Rangers in the semi-final, with Bobo Balde getting the Celtic goal. Scottish Cup duty was next on the agenda and and Larsson missed out on the quarter-final visit to Pittodrie, with Petrov and Hartson getting the goals in the 2-0 win and it was a similar story in the home league game against Aberdeen, with a Thompson penalty claiming the points for the Celts. Another Rangers game followed on March 10, with Petrov getting the Celtic counter in the 1-1 draw at Ibrox then the Bulgarian followed that up with the only goal in the 1-0 home win over Dundee United. Larsson was on hand with yet another double in the 4-0 away win over Motherwell and amazingly that set up the prospect of Celtic lifting their second successive championship almost a year to the day when they lifted their first title under Martin O'Neill.

The previous title was won on April 7, 2001, and Celtic's next league game was on April 6. There was, however, the Scottish Cup semi-final to be dealt with before then and Larsson added a goal to the double scored by Alan Thompson to give Celtic a 3-0 win over Ayr United at Hampden.

And so to the possibility of another championship party at Celtic Park. Livingston were the visitors and they had already voiced their disapproval at the proposed presentation of the championship trophy considering that Celtic still had to win the three points. It was pointed out that the organisation was nothing to do with Celtic and no disrespect was being aimed at the Lothian club. All the planning was in the hands of the Bank of Scotland SPL sponsors and Celtic knew fine well that Livingston could come and spoil the party. The Almondvale club did have a point, taking all things into consideration.

The previous season on championship day, Celtic played bottom of the table St Mirren and struggled throughout the game, only to win by a fluffed goal. Whereas this season Livingston had been the main challengers to the Old Firm throughout the season and would finish third in the table. Also, they were the first, and one of the few, teams to take points from Celtic during the season. Another argument would be that, along with Aberdeen, they were the only side to take more than one goal from Celtic during a game. Livingston had a fair point; there were still three points to be won but while a nervous Celtic struggled with St Mirren a year previously, a Henrik Larsson-inspired Celtic went to town this year round.

Larsson was in glorious form and his stirring play aroused one of the great Celtic displays of the season. Any nervousness or tiredness was discarded as confidence and energy oozed from every pore. The Magnificent Seven banged in his second hat-trick in seven games and John Hartson weighed in with a double for a 5-1 win and, for the first time in 20 years, Celtic had won back-to-back titles. The parties went on well into the night and at the end of the day even Livingston would probably see the sense in the SPL sponsors arranging for the trophy to be there. After all, as Martin O'Neill pointed out in the run up to the game, they could always take it away and bring it back. Celtic had another two home game in succession and Larsson was rested for the first, a 3-0 win over Dunfermline and returned for the following week's game with Rangers.

That Old Firm Derby finished in a 1-1 draw, with Alan Thompson scoring the Celtic goal as Celtic finished the SPL campaign unbeaten against their city rivals. The final two away games were Hearts (4-2) and

Aberdeen (1-0) meaning that Celtic had reached and surpassed the 100-point mark; they were the first team ever to amass 103 points in the league.

There was still the double to play for before the league was finally over, though, and the week before the final SPL game against Aberdeen, Celtic and Rangers met in the Scottish Cup final. Hartson and Balde scored in the Hampden showpiece but it was another day to forget for the Celts as Lovenkrands scored in the final seconds to present Rangers with a 3-2 victory and prevent the Celts from winning the double.

It was still a season to remember for Larsson and his Celtic team-mates, though. They had increased their points tally from 97 to 103, the goals for tally had gone from 90 to 94 and the goals against tally fell from 29 to 18. A truly remarkable improvement, considering the state the club was in before Martin O'Neill arrived in June 2000. Larsson had yet again finished top scorer and his final tally for the season was 35 but the goal ratio of young Shaun Maloney was also catching the eye. He hit three of his 10 goals in the final two SPL games of the season with Larsson absent from the team.

And since then the precocious and bullet-fast striker has signed a new contract but the youngster never had any doubts about staying on with Celtic despite the likes of Larsson ahead of him in the pecking order. He said: "I've never felt like leaving. Not at this stage because at my age I felt that I had to sign a new contract, as I was desperate to stay. There were players ahead of me like Henrik, John and Chris but, I always wanted to stay and put in a fight for my place because I think that there's going to be a place for me soon."

Maloney has joined that elite Celtic troupe of dead-ball experts who huddle around every long-range free-kick like vultures circling while a seemingly stranded goalkeeper looks on in fear. Will it be Maloney, will it be Larsson, Petrov or Thompson? They can all fairly strike a ball but who decides who is going to take it and what is said in the mini-huddle? Maloney said: "I would say that it goes on the confidence during the game, if I have just come on, which is pretty likely at the moment, then it's too soon for me. Then you've got people like Henrik hitting it and you've got Thompson who can hit a ball, Stan hasn't hit one in a long time but he can definitely strike it.

"So it's really whoever's confident enough and they can all do it.

So I'm sure if anyone turns around and says, 'yeah, I'll take it.' I don't think there's going to be anyone arguing with them. But they're not worked out at training. No, not at the minute. It's more about how you feel in the game, the thing about the training ground is that it's more relaxed and you don't mind missing, there's not 60,000 people screaming at you, badly wanting you to win, so it's basically talked about on the pitch."

He added: "It's difficult learning from someone like Henrik because you want to do the same things he does. At times you just fall short of that and you're just so desperate to be up at his kind of standard, be up close to him. And you want him to feel as if he's confident in you. It's like that with the rest of the team, I feel, because he is such a good player that in training you don't really learn that much. It's in the games that you see his movement. The amount of chances he gets to goals scored is quite striking really; he's definitely a one-off for the Celtic fans. And it's difficult for personal coaching during a game because obviously he's got to worry about his own performance. But at times, if we are up, or if maybe he feels that he's got something that I should be doing, he's got no problem about turning around and telling me.

"I'm the first person to tell you that I'm desperate to learn and when you've got people like Henrik in the team you've got to make the best use of them. He's certainly got that bit extra that I think all players want and, especially in my position, he's someone that I've got to keep learning from. As to how much I've learned from him, I don't know if I could really pinpoint one thing. But his movement on the park is unbelievable. There are defenders who think they've got him and they just realise that he's stepped back or he's made a run across them and his finishing is top-drawer. His one-touch finishing as well, and that's probably one of the things that I need to learn from him. A lot of it is instinct for him, I've asked him before if there are certain things I should be practicing and a lot of the time it's just the instinct and what first comes into his head.

"Like his goal in Hungary, he just turned and I don't think anybody really saw the keeper off his line but he just tried it because he had the confidence and that's when things start working out. Instinct is something you can't really teach, though. He does try his best to help me along the way and kind of teach me as many things as he can. But

I've got to take the responsibility and try and get up there and play alongside him. But it's the confidence thing as well, he's that confident in his own ability and I think every player will tell you if they're that confident, things are going to come off because you just try them and when that happens things seem to work for you."

Maloney added: "You never see him in the papers or anything like that with negative press. He's a very private man, I'm not saying that he's not friendly because he's obviously good friends with a lot of the team. He is a good role model that way; he's never really got these exclusives in the paper. He's just somebody that enjoys his football, enjoys being part of a team and when he finishes he goes back to his family and that's where he is. Not just as a football player but also as a person he is definitely a role model, for not just me but for probably every young player. I don't think you could find many weaknesses in his game and I'm definitely not going to sit here and try and pick them out. But he's somebody that if you look at, he can do a lot of things. I think the bottom line is that people have now realised, with what he's done in big finals and European Championships and World Cups, that he is a genuinely world class player."

So Larsson's goals had helped Celtic to back-to-back championships for the first time in 20 years and great strides had been made on the European front. The Swedish striker finished the season on the 156-goal mark for Celtic but could he reach the magical 200 figure the following season - or more to the point, would Celtic have the bonus of a long run in Europe to give him the leeway to reach such a total?

Chapter VI
Final score of the Swedish Rhapsody
But Larsson keeps on chanting the Celtic Song

THE look of your average football supporter has changed dramatically over the years. In days gone by, the punter who turned up on a Saturday very rarely sported the colours of his team. There is the image often seen on old, black and white Pathe newsreels of thousands upon thousands of cloth-capped, working-class men flocking to the terracings. There is also the endearing image of the bunnets, decades before Fergus McCann arrived, being flung in the air at the celebration of their team hitting the back of the net. Rosettes were the only favours and youngsters had football ricketies clacking away down the front. Any scarves worn were usually of the more sober variety and the football fan had altogether a rather quaint image compared to that of today. Cup finals were probably the only occasions in which the supporters would get more colourful, with outsized top hats in their team colours. Silver foil copies of the cup were held aloft on the terracings but Pathe always captured the action from the big games, the bread and butter games weren't nearly as colourful or vibrant.

Things gradually changed down the years though, scarves became de rigeur and plastic, blow-up Jimmy Johnstone dolls vied for space on the slopes with cut-out Scottish Cups. Supporters who actually wore football tops were very few and far between but now those who wear Celtic jerseys at the game generally outnumber those who don't. There is a wide variety of Celtic T-shirts and official casual tops in there as well, and over the past 15 years or so it had become no surprise that Republic of Ireland international tops have been dotted throughout the stadium to join the tricolours flowing in the wind. During the past seven years though, the merest tad of a blue element has been seen in the stands at Celtic Park - the blue trimming of the yellow Swedish international top and that had been partnered by the Swedish national flag seen flying side by side with the tricolour.

Larsson mania had swept in and suddenly, in the East End of Glasgow at any rate, the Scandinavian country became known for something other than Volvo, Abba or Ikea. Henrik Larsson was the biggest thing to hit Celtic Park in years, and, in marketing terms, the biggest thing ever. Rather strangely, Larsson is bigger in Scotland than he is in his homeland despite him being a national icon on the football front back home. There are two reasons for this, the Swedes as a people are slightly more undemonstrative than we are in Scotland and, despite the Swedish team's successes on the international stage over recent years, football just isn't all that big in Sweden.

As Denmark were the first mainland continental country to form a football association, they led the way in Scandinavia in the early years of the previous century. But even despite the re-emergence of the Danish national side in more recent years on the European front, even their football heroes vie with other sports such as handball for the devotion of their fellow citizens. However, in the 1920s, Sweden took over the mantle of being the top Scandinavian footballers as they brushed aside the Danes. The key reason for this, despite the Danes starting first, was the stronger club scene in Sweden. That has held more or less firm to this day with IFK Goteborg winning the UEFA Cup twice, the only Scandinavian club to do so. Gothenburg was the original centre of club football in Sweden and remains so to this day.

Football arrived there in the 1870s thanks to Scottish riveters and English sailors in Gothenburg and British embassy staff in the public parks of Stockholm. One wonders if any descendants of those Scottish riveters chant 'You are my Larsson" from the Celtic Park stands today. Swedish football's first governing body, the Swedish Sports and Athletic Association was formed in the city in 1895 to organise the burgeoning football clubs within Gothenburg. The first championship was open only to clubs from the city and Orgryte IS, formed there in 1887 and the oldest surviving Swedish club, lifted the inaugural title. As the 20th Century arrived, the tournament was opened up to include teams from Stockholm and two years later in 1902, an unofficial national body was set up there as the governing power base shifted. In 1904, Sweden joined FIFA as one of the founding members and a few months later the current Swedish Football Association was formed. The new governing body took over the championship which continued as a basic knock-out competition until 1925 when the national league was introduced.

Domination of the early years was shared by clubs such as original winners Orgryte and IFK, GAIS, AIK who would eventually produce Johan Mjallby, and Djurgardens. All of these clubs were based in either Gothenburg or Stockholm, and although IFK Eskilstuna became the first provincial club to win a championship under the old regime in 1921, it was not until the 1930s and '40s that other provincial clubs such as Helsinborgs IF (Henrik's old team), IFK Norrkoping and Malmo FF began to make inroads into the championship stakes. On the international front, the Swedes made their first appearance in July 1908 and they recorded the most impressive international debut to date by defeating Norway 11-3 in Gothenburg. Despite that resounding kick-off, they were to suffer at the hands of more experienced teams. For instance, their next two games against an England amateur select finished in 6-1 and 12-1 defeats. It wouldn't be until the 1920s that Sweden started to record international results of any regular significance.

But throughout the early years of their amateur internationals, it was to be Holland who were to be their nemesis. In the 1908 Olympics, it was the Dutch who robbed them of the chance of a third-place medal by winning 2-0 in London. The 1912 games were played on home ground in Stockholm but again the Dutch triumphed 4-3. In the 1920 games in Antwerp, the Dutch won 5-4 although the Swedes did manage to beat Greece 9-0 in the previous game. In the Paris Olympics of 1924, they eventually gained revenge on the Dutch and finally won the bronze medal by winning 3-1 after a 1-1 draw. Although football wasn't massive in Sweden, they were producing stars and two of the early heroes were Herbert Karlsson and Karl Gustafsson.

Karlsson must have been an early Larsson because he scored seven of those 13 goals in two games in the 1920 Olympics. Another Larssonesque figure was Sven Rydell; the Orgryte striker who scored 49 international goals in 43 games between 1923 and 1932 and that remains a Swedish record. Other early heroes were the likes of Harry and Alnin Dahl, Knut Kroon, Per Kaufeldt and Sigfrid Lindberg but this was all purely on an amateur level. These were the type of players who made Swedish football the best in Scandinavia but, ironically, Sweden toiled in the Scandinavian Championship which was played over a several-season period. Denmark won the 1924-29 tournament while the 1929-32 competition was won by Norway. It wasn't until the 1933-36 tourney that Sweden triumphed when many felt the team was inferior to their earlier contemporaries. The Swedes made their first serious impact in the World Cup of 1938 in France. They had a walkover in the first round when Austria scratched. They went straight into the quarter-finals and pretty much had a walkover there also when they defeated the lowly Cuba 8-0 in Antibes. In the semi-final they lost 5-1 to Hungary and then Brazil defeated them 4-2 in the play-off game.

Back on the domestic front, the Swedish Cup first saw light of day in 1941 when Helsinborgs became the first ever holders with a 3-1 victory over IK Sleipner. That national team which lost to Brazil in the World Cup play-off featured Sven Jonansson, Tore Keller and Eric Persson but the 1940s produced another trio of Swedish superstars when they at last won the Gold medal in the London 1948 Olympic games. Austria (3-0), Korea (12-0) and old foes Denmark (4-1) were seen off before they beat Yugoslavia 3-1 in the final.

Swedish football was catching the eye abroad and the attacking trio of Gunnar Gren, Gunnar Nordahl and Nils Liedholm were all snapped up by AC Milan and formed the famous Gre-No-Li forward line, where they no doubt came up against Faas Wilkes at the San Siro. The Swedes practiced the same amateur code as the Dutch and many Swedish exports were banned from playing for the national side. And as Swedish players were snapped up all over Europe, only two of that winning Olympic team, Karl Palmer and Nacka Skoglund, remained in Sweden and were eligible to play in the 1950 World Cup in Brazil. They topped the opening group by beating Italy 3-2 along the way but didn't fair so well in the next group, which included Brazil but they did finish third in the tournament overall. However, after defeating the then defending champions Italy, another six of those players were signed up by Italian teams.

Another departure to Italy, that of Kurt Hamrin, was viewed with as much disdain by the Swedes as the loss of Faas Wilkes was seen by the Dutch. The Swedish Football Association abandoned their policy of only selecting home-based players for international games - just in time for hosting the 1958 World Cup. They topped their group after beating Mexico and Hungary while drawing 0-0 with Wales. Their Stockholm base was also the venue for their 2-0 win over the Soviet Union in the quarter-finals while they moved to Gothenburg for the 3-1 win over West Germany in the semi-final. Stockholm hosted the final and the host nation had the misfortune to meet a Brazil side featuring the talents of a 17-year-old named Pele. The final score was 5-2 to the South Americans but the Swedish national team, featuring a host of players from the Italian league, were no longer a worthy but amateur team - and their class showed.

Much of the Swedes' success over that past decade was down to the work of George Raynor, their English manager. But when Sweden just failed to qualify for the 1962 World Cup in Chile after losing a play-off to Switzerland in Berlin, Raynor quit.

Swedish football was then in the comparative doldrums and it wasn't until the 1970s that it started to flourish once more. They qualified for three World Cups and produced great names such as Ralf Edstrom and Ove Kindvall who were both based in Holland - it was Kindvall who scored the deciding goal when Feyenoord defeated Celtic in the 1970 European Cup final. Another favourite was defender Bjorn Nordqvist who made 115 international appearances between 1963 and 1978, which was a world record at the time. These were the sort of players a very young Henrik Larsson could aspire to between watching the likes of Kenny Dalglish and Kevin Keegan on television. Swedish club football was on the rise too and Malmo FF reached the 1979 European Cup final where they lost to Martin O'Neill's Nottingham Forest. Gothenburg were to reach higher status and prove that part-time football didn't necessarily mean they were casual when it came to European trophies. They won the UEFA in 1982 beating Hamburg and again in 1987 against Dundee United. In 1986 the same side narrowly lost out on the European Cup when they lost on penalties to Barcelona.

This then was the developing football environment where the young Henrik Larsson grew up in the 1970s and '80s. Football still competed for exposure never mind the hearts of the people with sports such as ice hockey but Larsson's hometown of Helsinborg, like Gothenburg a 100 years earlier, was a football-crazy stronghold. And it was on the streets, playgrounds and public parks of Helsinborg that the future Swedish hero honed the skills that would have 60,000 singing his praises every other Saturday at Celtic Park. But how much of an icon is Henrik in the land of his birth?

The best man to ask would be his Celtic and Sweden team-mate Johan Mjallby. The big Swedish defender said: "Obviously in Sweden I would say we are bit more reserved and maybe football is not as big as it is here in Scotland. Over the years football has become quite big but Henrik is up there with the best ever Swedish players. He is an icon but I would say he is probably bigger over here in Scotland than he is in Sweden. That is possibly because in Sweden we are that bit more reserved. He's been voted the best Swedish player of the last 50 years, I think that's the proof that he's very well respected. Obviously he is better known back home now than he was before he joined Celtic. He popped up in the Swedish First Division when he was very young and he only played for two years in the top flight in Sweden before going to Feyenoord. So he disappeared from the Swedish view for a while but he played for the national team and at the time he was young.

"The manager we had at the time didn't really play Henrik in the USA World Cup. So obviously, since he moved to Celtic, we can all see that he has really, really matured to be one of the best players in the world. He has been so important for the Swedish national team and obviously for Celtic as well as we all know. I have to say that I think there were some doubts about him from the Swedish media when we went over to Japan to play in the World Cup. That was because they said that playing in Scotland was nothing special. They were saying now we have to see if he can bang in the goals that he has done over the years for Celtic. But he showed them straight away what a fine player he is and I think he is respected all over the world. And that was at the time he was coming back from his leg-break injury. He has shown that when we are playing games against the top teams in Europe, he is a proven goalscorer, but not only a goalscorer, he is one of the best and he is up there.

"For all of us it was a bit of a shock when he retired from international football, but he's such a well-liked guy. Everyone likes Henrik but he doesn't want to be in the limelight all the time, he just wants to prove himself on the pitch and that's why we all like him so much. Obviously it was a bit of a shock because he was the most important player over the past few years. But I think everyone respected his decision, and I think we can all understand that after playing for the national team for so many years then you might want to spend some more time with your family. Personally I think it's so hard to evaluate exactly where he stands in the list of all-time Swedish greats. Obviously I haven't seen the guys who played 30 or 40 years ago so it's hard for me to say but, as I said before, they had this poll and he got the number one post so that says it all. I mean he is the best I've played with during my years but I'll leave it to others to compare him with the players of yesteryear"

Mjallby added: "I think I played against him a couple of time when he was with Helsinborgs and I was with AIK before he moved to Feyenoord. Obviously we knew that he was a bright young striking star coming up but we only saw him for one or two seasons in the top flight. But he was so good and we could all see what sort of talent he was and obviously Feyenoord bought him quite quickly. He has matured and I think coming to Celtic was very good for him because he's always been a great player but Celtic gave him confidence. And confidence is very important for a striker. Banging in goals regularly for us like he has been doing shows that the confidence is up there all the time. He has proven himself against the best and he usually comes out on top so it's always been hard to play against him. But I think it's even harder nowadays as I rate him as up there with the best strikers in the world.

"It helped me that Henrik was at Celtic as far as settling in goes. That was one of the reasons why I came. There were other clubs interested in me at the time but it obviously helped having Henrik here, who I knew at the time after playing with him for the national team. Henrik being at Celtic had a bearing on me coming here, not everything obviously, but he helped me a lot for the first couple of months when I first moved over here because it's always a big step to move to another country and to a new club. We socialised away from the park. He showed me a lot of things and he told me what to do, how to set up things and sort stuff out. He was a big help, not only him but his wife Magdalena as well. We used to room together on international trips but in later years there was the choice of single rooms. Now you have the choice of single rooms and we are quite used to that from our time here as well. We shared a couple of times when we didn't have that option for the first couple of games but then we got tired of each other's snoring."

He added: "We all know that he is the big talisman and he is probably the most important player in the team. Not only for his goalscoring reputation, but also for his work-rate and obviously, without a player like Henrik, it would have been so much harder in a way to win anything never mind the treble. He trains like all of us but the thing about Henrik is that he loves football. He is the first one out there on the training pitch with a ball always; he always wants to have the ball. He doesn't want to run, he's not a keen runner but he can run for fun if he wants to, he's so fit it's unbelievable. But he loves football and he wants to be involved with the ball all the time, which is great. Even at his age, I mean he's still a young boy, but he's 32 and in football that's getting a bit older, he's still so fit and he loves being out there with the ball."

If Mjallby was shocked when Larsson decided to hang up his international boots, then spare a thought for Sweden's manager Lars Lagerback. The national boss said: "We miss Henrik badly, though. It goes without saying that we would still love him to be with us, but he has made his decision and I'm afraid it is one that he is now sure of. When Henrik goes, you don't just lose a goalscorer - you lose a very influential and positive character. We miss so much about him, and a lot of that is down to his personality and desire. He was someone that everyone in our squad respected and looked up to. With Henrik, you do not have a normal striker; he is a player who works incredibly hard in chasing back and making things difficult for the other team. We don't have another player who can do what he did for us, and not many teams do. In my opinion, he is unique, not only in Sweden but also in the world. If you look at other great strikers, they will maybe score as many goals as Henrik, but they do not work nearly as hard. That is what makes him so special."

Larsson did a 'Paul Lambert' when Lagerback approached him about returning for a vital game and the national coach was still holding out hope that the striker would change his mind again. He said: "We can always live in hope. He did a great job for us when we won a very important match in Hungary, and I wouldn't give up hope completely that he would come back. It's his decision, of course, but his presence alone lifts the whole team. He still hasn't made his mind up where he is going at the end of the season but if I were in charge at Celtic, I would do absolutely everything possible to try and get him to stay. He has said he will be leaving and, yes, Henrik can be very strong-willed about things like this when he knows what he wants. But nothing is impossible, and maybe leaving Celtic will be tougher than Henrik himself thinks. Celtic has definitely been great for Henrik - just as he has been great for Celtic. He has developed into a world class player in Glasgow, especially after coming back from his leg break, which was when he became truly exceptional. Winning the Golden Shoe was the highlight, an unbelievable achievement, and I'm sure Henrik will be remembered well in Scotland whatever what he decides to do."

As Johan Mjallby pointed out, the Swedish Football Federation nominated Larsson as the greatest Swedish player of the last 50 years. The offshoot of that is further entry to UEFA's 'Golden Player' award which will help commemorate the governing body's 50th anniversary.

Lagerback said: "This is very much a fitting honour for Henrik. Decisions like these are always difficult, and I think that it's almost impossible to compare a modern day player with someone from the great Swedish teams of 1958 or '74. But Henrik was a popular and worthy choice. I certainly can't think of anyone who has been more influential in Swedish football, and I believe that it is the right decision to put him forward for our nation. Sometimes the Swedes are quite slow to recognise their fellow countrymen in this sense, but watching Henrik follow up what he did for us at the World Cup with so many goals for Celtic in the UEFA Cup made everyone realise what a special player he is. Also, I think players are always appreciated more after they have gone, so in that respect he probably retired from the national team at the right time."

Larsson has scored 24 goals in his 72 international appearances for the Swedish national side. His international debut was a World Cup qualifier against Finland in Helsinki in October 1993. With the score tied at 1-1, Larsson hit the net to put the Swedes in the driving seat and they eventually won 3-1 - they qualified for USA '94 that day. Larsson played in that World Cup and it was in another such competition in Japan/Korea 2002 that it looked like his last international game would be played. Larsson had helped Sweden to a 1-1 draw with England, scored both goals in the 2-1 win over Nigeria, played in the 1-1 draw with Argentina and then scored against Senegal. It was then that he decided to give up the international scene until the plea arrived and he wore the yellow of Sweden once more against Hungary. That game was played on April 2, 2003 and Larsson helped the Swedes to a vital 2-1 away win. So Charles Wildman's 1948 classical piece Swedish Rhapsody had faded out to the final bar. But Larsson's decision to retire from the international scene meant his football concentration could be 100 per cent focused on Celtic - and that was no bad thing considering what was to transpire in season 2002/03.

King Henry the Fifth (Act III, Scene II)
"Men of few words are the best men."

The Bard, hardly a man of few words himself, couldn't have put it any more succinctly as Celtic's King Henke could hardly be described as a motormouth. Having one of the world's top players right on their doorstep would normally be a dream for the journalists who ply their trade within the realms of Scotland's back pages - not so with Larsson, though. He might have more than most to shout about but the King of Kings gives little if anything away. The football press like their subjects to be garrulous and gallus but in the world of Henrik Larsson talk is cheap. He does his talking where it matters - on the park - and it's only after the fact, after the damage has been done that he could be accused of having the most vicious tongue in football. Getting words from Larsson may be like getting blood from a stone but getting goals... well that's an entirely different story altogether and the Swede was once more going to do plenty of talking on the park in season 2002/03.

As with the previous season, the term kicked off with a league encounter and the raising of the championship flag. Dunfermline were the visitors and Larsson stated his intentions early in the best possible way by netting both of Celtic's goals in the 2-1 win. He showed that his World Cup exertions hadn't dulled his sharpness in any way whatsoever when he headed home a Bobby Petta cross four minutes before the break. Then, 20 minutes after the break he latched on to a Stilian Petrov flick to fire Celtic two in front. The flag raising and Larsson's two goals were made all the sweeter as Kilmarnock had held Rangers to a 1-1 draw at Rugby Park. Seven days later the Celtic team bus drew up outside Pittodrie and by the time it left a few hours later, Celtic were another three points and four goals to the good. The Swede didn't find the net this time but played a major part as goals from Johan Mjallby, Chris Sutton, Momo Sylla and Paul Lambert gave Celtic a 4-0 win.

Celtic again dipped their toes in the waters of the Champions League when the qualifying draw threw up old European foes, FC Basel. Things didn't look too great, though, when Christian Giminez put the Swiss ahead after only two minutes. Larsson levelled matter from the spot just a further two minutes later after Petrov was brought down in the box. Sutton and Sylla rounded off a fantastic night for the Bhoys as they carried a 3-1 victory through to the second leg in Switzerland. Dundee United were the next to feel the force as the Celts triumphed 5-0 with the goals shared by five players. Larsson hit the fifth and final goal in the 80th minute with a header following a cross from new Bhoy, Spaniard David Fernandez. A trip to Firhill to play Premier newcomers Partick Thistle followed, and the game proved to be a sluggish, long-drawn out affair and it was Larsson who separated the teams. His previous 160 goals for Celtic came from his left foot, his right foot or his head. This time, however, he opted to chest the ball in.

Celtic jetted out to Basel for their return Champions League leg but within 23 minutes, the dream was all but over. The Swiss side had scored two goals by then to level the tie on aggregate and they eventually won on the away goals rule. There was to be no Champions League adventure this year. Instead, the UEFA Cup beckoned.

The Bhoys, having been brought back down to earth with a bang by Basel, then played host to Livingston with Larsson being joined in the team by fellow Swede, keeper Magnus Hedman. Larsson set the ball rolling in the 21st minute with another header and Bobo Balde tied things up before the break for a 2-0 win. There was no game on the card for the following weekend but that didn't stop Larsson earning plaudits for his efforts in the green and white. More than 3,000 gathered in Glasgow's Armadillo auditorium for the Greatest Ever Celt night. Larsson was not only voted the Greatest Foreigner but he was also listed in the Greatest Ever Celtic Team. The full team was: Ronnie Simpson, Danny McGrain, Tommy Gemmell, Billy McNeill, Bobby Murdoch, Paul McStay, Bertie Auld, Jimmy Johnstone, Bobby Lennox, Kenny Dalglish and Henrik Larsson.

The following Tuesday could hardly be described as Celtic's greatest night, though, as they suffered their first SPL reverse of the season when three points were dropped at Fir Park. Motherwell went two ahead in the second half and though John Hartson pulled one back to make for a hectic finish, 2-1 was the final score. Hartson was again on target when Hibernian visited Celtic Park four days later but this time the full points quota was won thanks to that single goal. The Champions League exit was soothed somewhat by entry to the UEFA Cup and unknowns FK Suduva of Lithuania were paired with the Celts. Larsson bounced back with a triple bang in the goalscoring stakes. In a 15-minute first-half spree, he had bagged his hat-trick. His third meant he had equalled Ally McCoist's record of 21 goals for a Scottish team in Europe. There were a few grumbles in the stand as the Swede was subbed on the hour mark as Martin O'Neill was one of the many who were unaware that Larsson could leapfrog the former Rangers player. However, no one was complaining about the performance as the Celts romped to an 8-1 win with the visitors scoring in the very last minute.

Larsson kept the engine going the following Sunday at Dens Park when his 18th minute goal, a sublime effort from a Steve Guppy pass, gave Celtic a 1-0 win over Dundee and another three points. Yet another Larsson hat-trick in successive game at Celtic Park kept the home fans howling for more. This time Kilmarnock were the victims when he not only scored three, the last from the spot in the final minute, but turned goal maker again, with Chris Sutton netting the other two goals. Larsson would have to wait to surpass McCoist's European record as the Martin O'Neill flew out to Lithuania, fully intent on playing a shadow team in the UEFA second leg. The damage had been done in the first leg at any rate but Rangers were next up on the domestic schedule and no risks were taken. In any case, the fringe team still recorded a 2-0 away win over Suduva.

Old Firm day yet once more and Larsson came within a whisker of netting three home hat-tricks in a row - he scored two in the memorable 3-3 draw. The visiting side had taken the lead in the sixth minute through Mikel Arteta but Larsson was to equalise in deadly fashion. Another new Bhoy, recent signing from Hibs Ulrik Laursen, drilled a pass to Sylla and the Guinean fired in a cross which Larsson met with more than a degree of skill. In one movement he controlled the ball, swivelled away from his marker and unleashed a volley past Stefan Klos. Just 10 minutes after the break, the Swede bulleted a header home from a Stan Petrov cross and Celtic were in front. Ronald de Boer levelled for the Ibrox side just a minute later and then Shota Arveladze put them in front. But 10 minutes from the end, Chris Sutton fired in the equaliser and the honours were even.

An international weekend followed and Celtic's next action was a trip to Tynecastle on SPL duty. A 4-1 win for Celtic was the outcome, with all the Bhoys' goals arriving in the first-half, including another Larsson double. Sutton and Petrov had put the Celts 2-0 up by the ninth minute. Larsson's first was a close-range volley in the 36th minute and then, just three minutes before the break he produced another of his delicate chips for the fourth. When Celtic were paired with Inverness Caley Thistle in the League Cup, the alarm bells started ringing. Martin O'Neill was having none of it, though, and such was his confidence he rested Larsson from duty and the Celts paid no heed to the pre-match hyperbole regarding the previous debacle and won 4-2 on the night. Back on Premier League duty, the Celts travelled to East End Park and repeated their most recent away performance with another 4-1 winning scoreline. Larsson opened the scoring this time and Thompson, Petrov and Sutton added to the final outcome.

The win over Dunfermline set the Celts up nicely for their next tie but it goes without saying that this was going to be an altogether different prospect for the Celts. The UEFA Cup draw had thrown the Celts in with Blackburn Rovers and the spicy debate that always surfaces when the Auld Enemy meet at club level was added to by that fact that former Ranger Graeme Souness managed the Lancashire side. There was also the, by now, interminably boring accusation that Larsson couldn't do down south what he did up north with relative ease. In any event, the charismatic Swede shot down two birds with one plundered goal in the 85th minute. He not only answered the critics but the goal was his 22nd for Celtic in European football and he made the Scottish record his own by overtaking Ally McCoist. To be fair though, Blackburn had given Celtic as much of a testing time they have had from any team at Celtic Park. Not that the Celts were complaining at the end of the night, but that would have had a lot to do with the 'Men against boys' taunt, allegedly attributed to Souness, that emanated from the Blackburn dressing room after the match. It was a comment which would come back to haunt the English side.

Another home SPL game awaited after the high of the Blackburn UEFA Cup tie and the crowd gave the Celts a heroes' welcome when they took to the field to play Aberdeen. The Sunday service was silver-lined as the Magnificent Seven scored one in a magnificent seven. Welshman John Hartson took all the plaudits by firing in four of the goals in the 7-0 rout. But Larsson's free-kick two minutes before the break took his scoring run to EIGHT consecutive matches during which he scored 14 times. The No.7 was off target in the next match at Tannadice but that still didn't stop the Bhoys from picking up another three points in the 2-0 win over Dundee United with Hartson and Sutton doing the necessary.

Come Thursday it was time to sort the men out from the Bhoys as Celtic travelled to Ewood Park for the second leg of the UEFA Cup tie. Due to the changing room tittle tattle from the English side, this was a Battle of Britain with buttons on. The Bhoys had been fired up by the comments of a fortnight earlier and, after their performance at Celtic Park, Blackburn were brimming with confidence. There was also the point that Larsson's goal in the first leg was hardly a masterpiece but if

Blackburn wanted to see a classic Larsson calling card - they only had to wait until the 15th minute of the tie on their own patch. Larsson accepted a pass from Sutton as Hartson slipped on the wet surface and sped forward before releasing the most delicate of clips over Brad Friedel - 1-0 (2-0 on aggregate). In the 68th minute Stan Petrov took a corner and Sutton met it with his head - 2-0 (3-0 on aggregate). That's how it finished at the end and the dream continued - men against Bhoys indeed.

Ever since the 2-1 defeat by Motherwell, the Celts had trailed in the league as Rangers held a slender one-point lead. However, the Ibrox side drew 2-2 with Aberdeen at Pittodrie on the Saturday after Blackburn while the Celts were due to play host to Partick Thistle on the Sunday. Top spot was the prize up for grabs and the Celts were going to seize it with both hands. Former Celt Derek Whyte helped them along the way with an own goal in the 10th minute and Petrov was to make his mark on both sides of the break before Larsson struck again with one of his deadly finishes right at the death. The 4-0 victory put Celtic one point ahead of Rangers and Larsson's last-minute strike was Celtic's 2,000th Premier Division goal since its inception in 1975. A trip to Livingston followed and Larsson was to fire in the first two goals of the countdown to number 3,000. The first came from the spot n the sixth minute while the second was a low drive seven minutes from the end.

By now there were no easy teams left in the UEFA Cup and Spanish side Celta Vigo were going to prove a hard mountain to climb for the Glasgow Celts. But Larsson donned his climbing boots and yet again presented Celtic with a 1-0 home lead to take away in Europe. In the 52nd minute, Steve Guppy swung over a corner and John Hartson got the knock on. Larsson was there despite the presence of a strong Vigo defence to rise and head home.

Motherwell arrived at Celtic Park on the Sunday hoping that Celtic would be tired after their excesses. There was no chance of that but it did take Celtic until the second-half to find the net. Larsson got the opener in the 3-1 win and a midweek test at Easter Road was to follow. Larsson didn't find the net but Stan Petrov took care of business with the only goal of the game against Hibs and another three points were in the bag. Next up was the clash with Rangers at Ibrox and Sutton was to better his record for scoring the earliest Celtic goal in an Old Firm. He was to net the fastest Old Firm goal ever when the ball nestled in the

Rangers not after only 19 seconds. However, Rangers took a 3-1 lead before half-time and although John Hartson pulled one back on the hour mark, there was to be no way back for Celtic.

The Bhoys could at least take some consolation in the fact that they were taking a 1-0 lead to Vigo for their next game and it was to be a nail-biting night for the Celts - of both teams. Jesuli levelled the tie in the 24th minute, but in the 37th minute Hartson levelled on the night to put the Celts ahead once more on aggregate. The game was put on a knife-edge once more when Benni McCarthy scored nine minutes after the break but the Welsh striker's goal was to prove crucial as the Celts went through on the away goals rule - and they were in Europe beyond Christmas for the first time in 23 years.

On the domestic front, though, the cold December weather presented a slip-up in the title fight. The venue was Rugby Park and a 1-1 draw was all Celtic could muster against Kilmarnock, allowing Rangers to move four points ahead. The Christmas and New Year period threw up four tough games but Larsson was to score in all four. First up was Dundee and after Hartson had given Celtic a first-half lead, Larsson tied things up nine minutes after the turnaround when he nodded home a Didier Agathe cross at the far post. Boxing Day saw the visit of Hearts and a John Hartson hat-trick helped subdue the Edinburgh side who had scored twice before Larsson chipped in, quite literally with the fourth in the 4-2 win. Rangers lost 1-0 at Motherwell and the gap at the top was back down to one point. In Celtic's third home game in a row and the last of the year, Celtic played host to Dunfermline and a solitary Larsson goal was all that separated the sides. Celtic first-footed at Pittodrie in the final game of the quartet and Larsson's brave header in the 29th minute earned a goal but it was at a cost. Larsson received a head injury in scoring and he was taken off before Aberdeen equalised for a 1-1 draw.

After the winter break, the Celts returned once more to Scottish Cup action and St Mirren were the visitors on January 25. At half time, the score was still goal-less but Larsson struck with his 31st and 32nd goals of the season before Momo Sylla got in on the act with another for a 3-0 win over the Paisley side. The Celts then played their first SPL game for almost a month and eased back into the swing of things with a 2-0 win over Dundee United at Celtic Park. Both goals arrived in the first-half, with Hartson netting the opener and Larsson keeping up his goals tally on the half hour mark. That was the end of a six-game scoring run for Larsson in which he had netted seven times. The Swede wasn't to find the net in the next game against Partick Thistle at Firhill but a Chris Sutton double secured all three points. Next up, Dundee United made a quick return to Glasgow but Hampden Park was the destination this time in the semi-final of the League Cup. Larsson was back on goal duty again, with Bobo Balde netting the other two in a 3-0 win for the Celts and they were through to another final.

That was followed by a 2-1 home win over Livingston but the victory came at a cost. After just 17 minutes, Larsson received a sickening but accidental blow from Livvy defender Gustave Bahoken. The diagnosis for the Swede was a double jaw fracture requiring hospitalisation and plates and screws inserted during surgery. He was expected to be out for six weeks and that was a massive blow for the Celts. He had already scored 34 goals in 35 games that season and Celtic's next European tie, their first beyond Christmas in 23 years, was just around the corner.

The Larssonless Celts faced the might of Bundesliga side VfB Stuttgart and once more the pundits were to doubt Celtic's ability to progress in the UEFA Cup - just as they had done before Celta Vigo and ditto for Blackburn Rovers. The doubts obviously heightened with the absence of the Swedish hotshot but as far as the fans were concerned Celtic had eVery chance of going though. Yes, the 'V' factor had well and truly kicked in. Each of the teams Celtic had played in the UEFA Cup had a 'V' in their name - SuduVa, Blackburn RoVers, Celta Vigo and now VfB Stuttgart. Hardly the most scientific approach to booking up for a break in the sun but nonetheless, some wiseacre soothsayers were already trawling the Internet to find out the price of a pint in SeVille.

Celtic lined up against the German club on Thursday, February 20 without Larsson AND Hartson, with young Shaun Maloney starting up front. The doubters seemed to draw first blood when Kevin Kuryani put 10-man Stuttgart ahead in the 27th minute - they'd already had a man sent off. But the battling Celts were not to be denied. In the 35th minute Paul Lambert produced a breathtaking goal and just 10 minutes later Maloney showed composure to deal with an attempted German clearance to put Celtic into the lead. Then in the 68th minute, Stilian Petrov squeezed the ball in from the tightest of angles to give the Celts a 3-1 home win and another tasty continental takeaway.

Hartson was back in for the visit of St Johnstone on Scottish Cup business and in the absence of Larsson he took over the role of spot-kick expert twice. His two penalty conversions sandwiched a Jamie Smith goal for a 3-0 win and cup progression. Continuance in another cup was Celtic's next aim as the VfB Stuttgart second leg was scheduled for just a week after the first. The Bhoys knew it was going to be tough though. Would Kuryani's away goal prove to be just a fatal as FC Basel's in the Champions League qualifier when Celtic took the same 3-1 home scoreline abroad? It could well have been if it were not for an electrifying opening 15 minutes from the Bhoys. Alan Thompson headed the opener after only 12 minutes and just two minutes later Chris Sutton fired in number two for an amazing 5-1 aggregate lead. The Celts were home and dry - or so it seemed. With goals in the 37th, 76th and 87th minutes, the hosts reduced the aggregate score to 5-4 and although the mathematics ensured that the Celts couldn't lose on away goals it still made for a final few nerVy minutes. LiVerpool were the next UEFA opponents and the 'V' factor was still on.

Hibs then visited Parkhead and things were looking comfortable when John Hartson headed two goals in the first 25 minutes. Tom McManus pulled two goals back for the visitors, however, and that's the way it stayed until three minutes into injury time when Johan Mjallby rose to head home a corner that he had won and the last-gasp Celts won 3-2.

Winning games begets success and success begets more games. That's the nature of the game and the next four games were going to stretch Celtic to the limit. Rangers - Liverpool - Rangers - Liverpool. A tough quartet in anybody's book. The stuff that dreams are made of and the stuff that can shatter dreams. Rangers were first on the agenda in the Premier League and there was talk of an Indian sign being held over Martin O'Neill's head - Celtic hadn't defeated Rangers since Alex McLeish took over the management role from Dick Advocaat. That was blown completely out of the water though and the 1-0 scoreline did little to tell the whole story of a game that Celtic controlled from start to finish. John Hartson got the all-important goal in the 57th minute. Chris Sutton rose with Lorenzo Amoruso to challenge for an Alan Thompson cross. The big striker won the ball and his nod on was met by the Welshman who calmly cushioned the ball on his thigh before emphatically crashing it into the net. The result put Celtic three points behind the Ibrox side and the Bhoys had a game in hand. Before the end of the week Liverpool would be the next team to walk though the front doors of Celtic Park.

Larsson was back...and how! Gerard Houllier's team arrived as favourites but Henrik Larsson arrived back from injury and with just one minutes and 40 seconds on the clock he announced his arrival big style. Celtic were in front with less than two minutes on the clock as the Swede slotted home to prove that he was back firing on all cylinders - and he did it against another Premiership side. The Battle of Britain Mark II was on and although Martin O'Neill's former charge at Leicester, Emile Heskey, equalised, the Celts could take great heart from their performance that night. The tired Celts went straight into the next meeting, the League Cup final against Rangers at Hampden Park. But this was the hardest of hard luck stories as a surprisingly energetic Celtic side took the game to Rangers but amazingly found themselves 2-0 down after 35 minutes. In the 56th minutes hopes were raised when Larsson headed in yet another goal. Just six minutes later it looked like the Celts were back on level terms when John Hartson slotted home but the linesman flagged for offside when the Welshman was clearly a yard onside. The Bhoys battled on, though, and despite Neil Lennon's sending off there was further hope when the Celts were awarded a penalty. Hartson sent the keeper one way and the ball the other but unfortunately it trickled past the post and the chance of the first trophy of the season was gone. There was further agony when it was announced that the injured Chris Sutton could be out for up to six weeks.

This was the big one. Celtic had been here before. Larsson had been here before. Back in Larsson's first season with Celtic, another memorable performance against Liverpool resulted in a score draw being taken down to Anfield but a 0-0 tie there burst Celtic's bubble and they went out on the away goals rule. Would the same thing happen again? Could the same thing happen again? Or would the 'V' Factor hold sway. The 'V' Factor had diddly to do with it. Alan Thompson, John Hartson and a magnificent Celtic performance held sway. As the first-half was coming to a close, Celtic were awarded a free-kick after Traore's pull on Larsson. With injury time ticking away, Thompson weighed up his options and fired in a daisycutter that went under the wall and into the net. Liverpool would have to score twice now but

Celtic weren't going to give them the opportunity and Hartson atoned for his Hampden penalty fluff when he exchanged passes with Larsson before firing in an unstoppable shot right into the top corner. Celtic were in the UEFA Cup semi-final and they certainly weren't going to walk alone.

Celtic were burning the candle at both ends, though, and just three days after returning from Liverpool they flew up to the rather more basic surroundings of Inverness Caley's Caledonian Stadium. Another fringe side took to the field in this Scottish Cup tie but once more the former Highland League side knocked the Celts out of the cup. For only the second time that season the Celts had failed to find the net as they went down 1-0 to Caley. With Rangers ahead by six points but the Celts having two games in hand things didn't look so bad. That is until another slip up, this time at Dens Park where Celtic took the lead through Alan Thompson but Dundee hit back through former Celt Mark Burchill for a share of the points. The two most recent domestic games hadn't been the most memorable but the players and supporters looked forward to the next European game - the UEFA Cup semi-final against Portuguese side Boavista - the 'V' Factor was still with us and SeVille could be only two games away.

For the first time in 29 years, Celtic Park played host to a European semi but the prospects looked bleak when a cruel and unlucky own goal by Joos Valgaeren put the visitors in front just three minutes after the break. Celtic had already had a couple of stick-on penalty claims turned down by then so our luck just didn't seem in. But when danger lurks all you have to do is call the Super Swede and within two minutes Celtic were back on level pegging. Neil Lennon and Stan Petrov were involved in the move that Larsson finished by slotting home from close range. In the 75th minute Celtic were awarded a penalty but the keeper palmed away the Swede's spot kick. The final score was 1-1 and Celtic could expect a tough time of it in the away tie in Oporto.

After the tiring Euro game and their recent domestic showings, Celtic could probably have expected a tough time of it when Kilmarnock visited a few days later but it didn't turn out that way. Larsson set the ball rolling with a powerful volley in the 20th minute and Stan Petrov tied things up in the 72nd minute for a 2-0 win. A trip to Tynecastle loomed and things seemed to be going to plan when Larsson latched on to and converted a Didier Agathe cross just before the hour mark but

Hearts equalised in the 72nd minute. Then, in the 90th minute, Austin McCann struck with a wonder goal and another three points were dropped. That left Celtic eight points behind Rangers but still with a game in hand.

From Tynecastle to the Estadio Do Bessa in Oporto. That was the Celtic schedule and the Bhoys had to lift themselves after the Hearts defeat or face falling at the penultimate hurdle in Europe. Celtic were on the verge of their first European final in 33 years and the squad were tired. But the will to win shone through and with 78 minutes on the clock the fairytale continued as Larsson struck yet again - just when it seemed that Boavista's apparent ploy of sitting on their shaky away-goal advantage may just work. The left foot of Larsson struck gold and Celtic supporters throughout the world had to endure the longest 12 minutes of their lives. We were there though; Larsson's touch had taken Celtic to the UEFA Cup final in Seville.

There were still domestic chores to be taken care of and the trip to Ibrox just three days later was turned into a massive beach party by the 7,000 or so Celtic fans who managed to get tickets. Beach balls, sombreros, shades, sun cream, lilos, donkeys, flippers, snorkels, water rings, buckets and spades, passports, macho moustaches, you name it, this holiday snap had everything except the lost luggage. Amid all the hilarity a match broke out on the park but even here the Beach Bhoys were surfin' as Alan Thompson and John Hartson gave the Celts a 2-0 lead. Rangers pulled one back in the second-half but Celtic had already kicked sand in their face. That left Rangers with 87 points while Celtic had 82 but the Bhoys had still played a game less. The following Saturday Celtic travelled to East End Park and Larsson got the first in a 4-1 win. The following day Rangers drew 2-2 with Dundee at Ibrox. Celtic then travelled to Motherwell in midweek and duly won 4-0 to go level pegging on points with the Ibrox. The Celts followed that up on Saturday with a 1-0 win over Hearts while the following day Rangers beat Kilmarnock 4-0 at Ibrox. On Wednesday, May 14, one week before Seville, Celtic beat Dundee 6-2 with Larsson again getting on the scoresheet while the following weekend saw Rangers defeat Hearts 2-0.

All roads led to Seville, though. Celtic supporters flew in from all over the world and made base camps in all parts of the Iberian Peninsula. They partied for nigh on a week all over Spain and Portugal and converged on Seville in droves as the kick-off time neared. Some reports say over 70,000 Celts were there, some say 80,000. But who knows? A Seville police inspector later reckoned the Celtic contingent to be over 115,000. But it didn't matter how many were there - the tickets weren't like gold dust, fanatical Celts were giving away gold dust for the tickets. There had quite simply never been a European final like this. Seville was overwhelmed and the Sevillians took the Celts to their hearts. But at the end of the day there was still a football match to be played and in the bursting, strength-sapping heat Celtic took to the field against Porto. The bare bones of the match are well known. Derlei gave Porto the lead just before the break. Celtic hit right back when Larsson headed in just two minutes after the restart. Alenichev put Porto back in front in the 54th minute. Larsson headed home yet again to make it 2-2. The game went into extra-time. Five minutes into extra-time Bobo Balde was sent off. Five minutes from the end, Derlei scored again and it was 3-2 to Porto.

Larsson had scored two goals in a European final and in doing so had scored his 200th goal for Celtic. That he flew home to Glasgow with nothing to declare at customs but a runners-up medal was a tragedy in the extreme. The Celtic backroom staff tried to console the battle-weary players but it was akin to trying to comfort a mourner at a funeral when all they want to do is shove you away and be alone. But they couldn't be alone with over 100,000 fellow Celts surrounding them. And they will never be alone. They will never walk alone.

The heartbreak of Seville had to be pushed to one side as the feint hope of three-in-a-row still rumbled. Celtic were playing Kilmarnock at Rugby Park. Rangers were playing Dunfermline at Ibrox. Both sides had 94 points. Rangers had scored 95 goals for the loss 27 with a goal difference of 68. Celtic had scored 94 goals for the loss of 26 with a goal difference of 68. It couldn't be any closer. Rangers had nosed in front by virtue of goals scored - 95 to 94. As the afternoon unfolded the destiny of the title would be decided. The long and the short of it is that Celtic won 4-0 while Rangers won 6-1 and the timing of the goals was such that the Celts never topped the table at any time throughout the next 90 minutes.

At the end of the day, Celtic lost the title by a goal difference of 73 to 72. Even if Rangers hadn't got their last-minute penalty we would still have lost on goals scored. Celtic had fought their way through 60 matches that season and in only two of them did they fail to find the net. It was a sickening end to a season in which so many dreams unfolded and very nearly came true. But the supporters were proud of their Bhoys and more that anything they were proud of Henrik Larsson.

Chapter VII
And so the end is near
Larsson will do it his way

THE season just past had been a remarkable, exciting but ultimately heartbreaking series of breathtaking adventures for Henrik Larsson and Celtic Football Club. From the opening day, when captain Paul Lambert and chairman Brian Quinn unfurled the flag and Henrik Larsson scored Celtic's first goal of the season in the 2-1 win over Dunfermline, right through to the excruciating tension and anxiety as the season came to an unimaginable close in the dying minutes of season 2002/03 on May 25 at Kilmarnock's Rugby Park.

Who would have thought back on August 3 when Larsson headed in that goal that the Celts would reach the final of a European competition? Who would have thought that while controversy raged over the Old Firm joining the English Premiership that Celtic would dispose of Graeme Souness' Blackburn Rovers and Gerard Houllier's Liverpool with more than a modicum of style, panache and glory? Who would have thought that another Scottish Cup defeat by Inverness Caledonian Thistle would have been viewed by many as nothing more than blip on the screen and not a calamitous bell-ringing emergency? And who would have thought that, despite losing the league to our oldest rivals in the final minutes of the season by the tightest of margins, it would still be just one amazing chapter of an extraordinary story wrapped in glory? Who would have thought that winning nothing would mean so much and so little?

The highs and the lows were indistinguishable. They were wrapped up in one big green and white ball for ultimately, the highs were the lows and the lows were the highs. There are few, if any, Celtic supporters who would have swapped the run to Seville and all that went with it for winning the championship – even if we had to forfeit the title to Rangers as well as relinquish the hopes of three-in-a-row. The sacrifice at the altar of European progression was deemed worthy enough to shrug off losing the title for just one more year. That's easy to say with hindsight, though. Would we have settled for that as Celtic kicked off against Dunfermline at the outset? Probably not. Instead of shrugging off the title for one more year we would probably have elected give the European scene a bye as Celtic were still on the upward spiral in continental terms, still learning with plenty of time for further education.

Many would have seen reaching a European final so soon after Martin O'Neill's arrival as little more than a pipe-dream and pipes have an awful habit of bursting during the winter months. The option of European glory could wait. Give us the championship. Give us three-in-a-row. Hadn't we waited 23 long years since we last progressed in Europe beyond Christmas? Hadn't we already waited 32 long years for a bite at the cherry of a European final? Hadn't we waited 35 long years since our last experience of swallowing the whole cherry? Surely we could wait one more year, as we certainly didn't want to abandon the title to Rangers of all teams. But those theoretical answers to hypothetical questions did not take into account the sight, the sound or the spine-chilling and tear-jerking spectacle of a vast green and white army descending on the picturesque southern Spanish town of Seville.

Just 10 months after Larsson knocked in that bread and butter goal against Dunfermline, the invasion and occupation of Seville not only upped the ante for the European coalition, it blew the championship alliance right out of the water. In the first 113 years or so of the Scottish League, 11 teams have won the championship and many more have had the opportunity but only ONE has taken 100,000 fans or more abroad to a European final. That one team was Celtic Football Club. We fight it out with Rangers regularly on an annual basis, but European finals don't come along too often. They have to be fought for and in getting there you have to fight against the best teams around, an experience that domestic football rarely gives occasion to. Celtic went through a learning experience in season 2002/03 and received a university education while still studying in the kindergarten of Scottish football and they graduated with honour. The SPL may be a primary school compared to the Oxbridge learning faculties of the likes of the Premiership, La Primera Liga, Serie A and the Bundesliga but this Celtic side passed all the exams and just failed by the merest of margins to make it to top of the class. In 60 games that season the Celts only failed to score in two, FC Basel (A) and Inverness Caley (A), and they managed to score 145 goals along the way. The Celts only lost 45 goals giving them a goals difference tally of a clear century and one of the major reasons for that difference was none other than Henrik Larsson who hit the net no fewer than 44 times that glorious season. Many of those goals were crucial, especially those on the European stage, and it is clear that, without Henrik Larsson, there would have been no Seville stories to regale the grandchildren with.

And it's also equally evident that the road to Seville couldn't have been mapped out without having Martin O'Neill at the helm. The Irishman was tailor-made for the Celtic job and he had been one of the many names quoted when the post was made available prior to season 2000/01. But much to the delight of Celtic fans throughout the world he did finally arrive to begin his assessment of the team at the start of what was to turn out to be the glorious treble season. Right away he had to start analysing the strengths and weaknesses of the squad at his disposal. There were obvious deficiencies in the playing pool, there were aspects that just had to be tweaked slightly and there were players that coaches dream about managing – then there was Henrik Larsson.

O'Neill said: "I can't say that I knew Henrik personally but obviously I had heard great things about him. At that time in June of 2000, of course, he was recovering from his broken leg, he was just going in to Euro 2000 and even though he obviously wasn't properly match fit he was going to be playing for Sweden. So with all of those things combined, I spoke to our club doctor, Roddy Macdonald, who told me Henrik had done wonderfully well to get fit. Roddy said that Henrik was really single-minded and that he never wasted a week during his rehabilitation. Once he had come to terms with the injury he was totally focused on getting fit as soon as possible. Obviously the great incentive for him was to get fit and try to play for Sweden in that particular competition but just as obviously he'd have liked to have been fitter. But all of those things combined to give me a bit of an insight into Henrik and I got to know him through part of the pre-season and it continued on from there.

"Naturally, I remember his opening goal in my time at the football club against Dundee United that particular Sunday. Chris Sutton ended up adding the other goal and it was wonderful win. And that was the start of it in my time. But, of course, he had been doing that for quite some considerable time beforehand.

"I think that he has a really fine ability to score a goal. That is a great gift never mind anything else. But one of the things I remarked on early was his ability to hang in the air. And for one who is only relatively tall and quite slender, he had this ability to hang in the air and be an excellent header of the ball in goalmouth situations. In other words, that taught me a lot about him. And you have to realise I've a great affection for people who can head the ball and certainly head it goalwards. It's something I'm always talking about it and it's a delight for me and us all that Henrik has that ability. That's something I hadn't realised was certainly part of his game. The other aspects of his game, the Celtic fans had come to appreciate before, I was exactly the same as soon as I watched him play.

"As far as managing Henrik goes, he is really the same as most of the players here. Generally speaking, he would have an opinion but very manageable in the sense that, regardless of who would be the manager at the football club. Quite a number of these players, including Henrik, would get down and work for anyone. So because they are focused, and that covers a number of things, they have their own ambitions and their own desires. And I think that Henrik is one of those boys that it wouldn't matter a jot to them who was managing the team, you would still be getting these excellent performances from him."

As O'Neill pointed out, he had arrived as manager when Larsson was just returning from his nightmare leg-break of the previous season but he was delighted as were all Celtic supporters, when it looked like the Swede was not only back to fitness, but maybe even back better than ever. The King of Kings started firing in goals from all angles and was instrumental in attaining the treble in O'Neill's first season in charge at Celtic. A total of 53 goals that season while winning the European Golden Shoe award for his 35 league goals (against all the odds as goals in the SPL receive a lower point rating than those in the top European leagues) certainly pays testament to that fact. Another fantastic spate of net-rustling the following season ensured that O'Neill's Bhoys secured their second successive championship as the Celts steamrolled to the title.

And the Swede maintained his unique scoring prowess as the Celts entered their third season under O'Neill when, even into March 2003, they were still battling it out in four competitions. But on February 9, it looked as if the wheels may fall off the apple-cart. Livingston visited Celtic Park and in trying to head for goal early in the game, Larsson clashed heads with Livvy's Gustave Bahoken and Celtic

Park fell silent. It looked bad. Larsson inched off from the pitch in obvious pain and despite giving the thumbs up to his wife Magdalena sitting in the stand, the Celtic crowd couldn't help but cast their minds back to October 21, 1999 when the Swede was stretchered off in Lyon and the rest of Celtic's season was in tatters.

Prior to the visit of Livingston, Larsson had already amassed 34 goals that season and many of them were truly vital. None more so than his goals against Blackburn Rovers and Celta Vigo in the UEFA Cup when his strikes made an invaluable difference to Celtic's European hopes. And just days after the Livingston match, Celtic were to play VfB Stuttgart in the next round of their European adventure. But Larsson had sustained a fractured jaw and was out of the proceedings.

O'Neill recalled: "What was going through my mind at the time was I was hoping that when he was taken of the field it wouldn't be as serious as it seemed. Roddy Macdonald soon informed me that it wasn't good news. I thought we were battling away against Livingston that day, finally winning a brilliant game coming from behind in the match. But right at that particular time the other picture was, and I knew how Henrik would be irritated with it because of the European games coming up, he would miss the Stuttgart games. So the rest of the team's disappointment at that stage would mirror his disappointment. Henrik ended up missing those games and at that stage any big player missing from that level of competition should lessen your chances of getting through. Maybe Henrik thought that because we were doing so well in the competition and coming up against one top class team after another, that the Stuttgart ties might be the final European games that we would be playing that season. Thankfully, young Maloney came in and did magnificently well, then the two centre forwards played so well together out in Stuttgart so we got through. So by the time Henrik came back we were still in the UEFA Cup."

The injury wasn't as bad or as long-lasting as the Lyon leg-break but O'Neill looked back on Larsson's rehabilitation from 1999 through to 2000 and said: "Lots of players come back from serious injury. The more courageous the player the less consideration he gives it, it's part of the game. Stilian Petrov broke his leg and was obviously inconsolable early on in the first couple of days. He felt, as all players do, that this might be the one that does your career in. I can understand all of those things. From my own personal experience of wrecking my knee I know exactly what players are going though at these times. You ask yourself is this the last time that you'll actually don a football shirt? It does enter your head regardless of what happens. There are many questions going through your mind. What happens if the break is compounded? Not just the break itself but what happens if the rehabilitation doesn't go to plan? All of those things go through your head but you need to be a strong character in those early days. Once you settle into a routine of getting back and you're getting reassurances from the doctor and all the medical team that everything is going to be fine, then that reassurance carries you on. And Henrik will be no different to Stan or anybody else in that aspect. Those reassurances do help you enormously."

In a long and illustrious club career as a player, O'Neill played with many great strikers as the Nottingham Forest side of the late 1970s and early '80s blazed an unexpected but highly successful trail through the upper echelons of English and European football. O'Neill and his team-mates, under the tutelage of the mercurial Brian Clough, were sweeping all in front of them as they comprehensively turned round the fortunes of the provincial club. And the strikers played no small part in that transformation and the success it yielded. But how does Larsson compare to the productive hitmen that O'Neill played with?

The manager said: "At club level when I was a player we had different types of centre forward. We had Peter Withe who, at Nottingham Forest, was absolutely terrific and when we won the championship I thought was sold prematurely by Brian Clough. Garry Birtles was a centre forward with really great ability. Trevor Francis was absolutely outstanding. Tony Woodcock was terrific. All had different aspects but Trevor Francis would be by far the quickest of all the ones I've just mentioned, even including Henrik. Trevor Francis was lightning and that was a big, big asset to him. Tony Woodcock was all left foot and when he got into trouble he turned to John Robertson and got help just by laying the ball off to him. But they were all very good players in their own right. Henrik is in that category. He has different aspects, he could head it as good as any of them, better in the air than a few of them. And while he's not the quickest player over 20 or 30 yards that you will ever see, the fact is that his brain is working all the time. And that's always the sign of any good centre forward. Quick-thinking, quick-witted and an eye for goal. Those centre forwards that I'm talking about all had that eye for goal. But what sets Henrik apart from other strikers is that when you consider top quality players in Europe, then Henrik comes into that consideration.

"That speaks volumes for him. You're looking at the strikers just now who are getting worldwide acclaim and you're talking about Thierry Henry and Ruud van Nistelrooy, who are definitely wonderful, wonderful footballers. Van Nistelrooy would probably score more goals than Henry but Henry is capable of going past any given player at any given moment in any given game. Van Nistelrooy can turn people and they are two totally different players, but both would be able to play with each other with absolutely no problem. I believe that Henrik could play with any of those two. He's got that ability to do so and I'll tell you what really sets him apart, he's got good enough individual talent to stand on his own and he's also a very good team member."

When Martin O'Neill joined Celtic though, Henrik Larsson's strike partner was already on his way out before the manager could do anything about it. Mark Viduka was on his way to Leeds United and the new manager had to act quickly to fill the gap up front. Especially as no-one, not even Larsson himself, no matter how much belief he had in his own mind, knew that the Swede would automatically return to top form within the blink of an eye. With that in mind the new manager wasn't particularly going shopping for a striker who would naturally compliment Larsson and play to the Swede's strengths. He knew that a fully fit Larsson could play with any striker and he was looking for another hitman with that same professional quality, that ability to link up with anyone no matter what the situation – another player who could stand on his own right but be fully committed within the framework of a team unit. He got it right first time and Chris Sutton's rancour at Stamford Bridge turned to splendour in Paradise.

O'Neill recalled: "At the time Viduka was going out the door, he had had enough and the deal was very much done before I arrived. From then on in it was just a matter of Celtic trying to get as much as we possibly could from the deal. When that situation developed we were then looking for a centre forward. I can't turn around and say that I was working specifically in getting someone in mind to partner Henrik. It would be incorrect to say that. I obviously had a thought as to what might help Henrik but I took Chris Sutton first and foremost because I thought he was a very, very good centre forward. He was much maligned at Chelsea but I saw his ability as a kid at Norwich and I watched him develop at Blackburn Rovers to be a very good player. He didn't do well at Chelsea and there are a number of reasons for that but I didn't for one minute think ability was one of them.

"Viduka is a different type of player to both Sutton and Henrik, maybe he's a bit more like Henrik rather than Sutton. But when I knew we were getting £6million for Viduka I thought if we could get Chris Sutton for the same amount of money then eventually he would prove his worth. And I'm delighted that he did do. It would be incorrect though to assume that I was looking for a striker specifically to partner Henrik – it is my belief and I do believe that top quality players can play with anyone if they have got their mind set to do so."

The partnership has proved to be made in heaven and O'Neill's philosophy has proved to be spot on. Right on the button, in fact, with Sutton, who has also dropped back in to midfield and defence with marvellous effect on many occasions, and the big Englishman has been a vital ingredient in the team's success under the Irish manager. Larsson, too, has proved the manager's point over the last three years in particular in forming just as lethal partnership with John Hartson and Shaun Maloney as he does with Sutton. It would seem that Larsson is the perfect role model for the modern game. From young kids playing in school playgrounds on to young professionals starting their careers with clubs like Celtic, right through to experienced professionals.

Such is his attitude to training as well as the 90 minutes on the pitch he is the perfect blueprint for any aspiring footballer as, despite the gruelling schedule in season 2202/03 when he played in 51 games, he only received one yellow card throughout the entire term. That's an amazing statistic when one considers the treatment dished out by defenders to a player of Larsson's obviously lethal threat. O'Neill said: "In terms of role models he's as good an example to kids as possible. He gets on with the game, seldom argues, will occasionally, in a bit of frustration, either gesticulate or say a few words, who doesn't? But the very fact is, his disciplinary record is absolutely excellent considering the amount of times he actually gets kicked in the game, as forwards tend to get kicked, then you would say that he's as good a role model as anyone in the game."

King Henry the Sixth, Part II (Act IV, Scene I)
"Small things make base men proud."

So said the Duke of Suffolk to the sea captain and Walter Whitmore in Shakespeare's obsession with all things Henke. That quote and the pre-empting line "O that I were a god, to shoot forth thunder upon these paltry, servile drudges!" could have been penned by our own King Henke as the night of May 21, 2003 drew to a close in Seville. To countless thousands of Celtic fans Larsson is a god. And he did shoot forth thunder twice from the golden crust of his head. Could the paltry, servile drudges be the Porto team who bowed down and paid servitude to the cruel and pitiful edict which states that wasting time and feigning injury can yield silver?

If these made the base men of Porto proud then so be it, but the 'small thing' in Henrik's case constitutes the runners-up medal he was presented at the end of over 120 minutes of muscle-stretching football that deserved so much more. To score twice in any game and still lose must be a sickener, but to do it in a European final at the tail end of a long and arduous season is truly mind numbing and heartbreaking. We all felt the loss that night. The players and management felt it even more. And the scorer of the two goals? Only he knows how he really felt that night. But manager Martin O'Neill suffered a similar experience when Nottingham Forest reached their first European Cup final against Malmo in Sweden back in 1979. When Forest manager Brian Clough read out his team selection for that night the name of Martin O'Neill was missing. So maybe the Celtic manager knows more than most the feeling of despondency experienced by Larsson that night. O'Neill said: "First of all, that was not just a disappointment to Henrik, it was to everyone. And it was always remain a disappointment because despite the memorable couple of days that the Celtic fans made it in Seville, the overhanging thing was that we actually lost the game. And that doesn't melt away with time. Henrik was as disappointed as anyone. At least he drew comfort from the fact that he played excellently in the game. But the fact is that playing excellently in a final is one thing, winning it is something else. Wouldn't it have been the perfect combination to have done both? And I'm quite sure Henrik would be the first person to say he would give up any of those two goals if we had actually won the game. If anyone had any doubts about him doing it on the Euro stage, that performance would have made people think again."

It's a fair enough assumption that Larsson's decision to give up international football with Sweden after appearing in two World Cups has played no small part in the continued success of Celtic. Fresh legs and an alert mind are more conducive to the week-in-week-out conveyor belt of club football rather than weary and bruised legs and a mentally tired player after yet another cross continent flight. It would also be a reasonable assumption then that Martin O'Neill felt the exact opposite as Swedish coach Lars Lagerback when Larsson decided to hang up his yellow and blue shirt. Surprisingly, that isn't the case and O'Neill, although wary of international excesses, loves seeing his players gain the recognition of playing for their country.

The Celtic manager said: "No, I can't say that I took any great delight in Henrik retiring from the international scene. It's the same with all my international players going away. I've never prevented anyone here playing for their country. It's a great, great honour. Of course, I'm a club manager and I'd prefer if they came back here in one piece. That's not always the case, though. We've lost a few in my time here – Paul Lambert, Jackie McNamara, Joos Valgaeren. That's costly to the club manager but in truth no, if Henrik feels that he has benefited from it in terms of feeling a bit fresher throughout the whole of the season that's fine. If he feels that he misses international football so much that he wants to go back then that's entirely up to Henrik. I would never ever try to talk him out of it. It was the same when Paul Lambert spoke to me about going back with the Scotland squad when Berti Vogts wanted him to return from international retirement."

Lars Lagerback may or may not be trying to tempt Henrik back to the international scene but far more important than that in the eyes of Celtic fans was Martin O'Neill's first contract talks with Henrik to persuade the Swede to stay with Celtic by extending his stay. Thankfully it would seem that O'Neill's powers of persuasion didn't need to be all that great. O'Neill said: "Of course I was delighted. I think we were all very, very pleased. When I first mentioned to Henrik that I'd like to sort the thing out, from that to the actual signing of the document seemed to take an age but it wasn't really. There were no severe arguments or anything like that. You want to pay the player his worth in the circumstances and it was only right that we do something for a player who had done a heck of an amount for the club"

The need for the talks were obvious in the case of a player of Larsson's outstanding ability for two reasons. Firstly he is a more than valued member of the Celtic squad and, secondly, there are always more than a few clubs sniffing around when the name Henrik Larsson arises and in mid-2003, Tottenham Hotspur were just the latest in a long line of clubs linked with the Swede. O'Neill said: "Its only natural that teams are going to come in. They look at a player like Henrik and find out that he's got one year left on his contract. They might think they can get him on the cheap or they might think they can get him by paying a fortune. The truth of the whole matter is that if Henrik really wanted to go we wouldn't and couldn't have stopped him. My policy is, if someone is really unhappy at the football club I'd like to get to the bottom of it and find out why. If I cannot after that be able to change someone's mind and he wants to go, then we try and get the best possible deal out of it for the football club. It never went that far because Henrik really wanted to stay. The truth is that players hold sway these days, I just don't mean Henrik. And if they really want to leave a football club they could make enough fuss of it and go, Thankfully that never happened in Henrik's case."

King Henry the Fourth, Part II (Act III, Scene II)
"Uneasy lies the head that wears the crown."

Thus spake Shakespeare's King Henke himself when he was having trouble getting a bit of shut-eye, and one wonders has our own modern-day King Henke ever had any sleepless nights pondering his future at Celtic? Or does the crown rest easy on his regal brow? The papers have been awash with what Henrik might do next and not a day goes by without Celtic fans wondering what their hero has decided. Has he even decided? The options are open for him and when you have the skill and expertise in front of goal that Larsson possesses then your choice is many and varied. The new season of 2003/04 dawned and it still remains to be seen if this will be Larsson's last with Celtic – maybe that will depend on how the club do in Europe this season, maybe it will depend on how we do domestically. Who knows? Maybe Henrik himself doesn't even know. One option is giving up football entirely – you never know with Henrik. He has stated that he would like to finish his playing career back in Sweden, preferably with Hogaborg, his very first club. But will that be at the end of this season or another two or three years down the line? Qatar has been mentioned in dispatches and with the oil-rich sheiks bandying Roman Abramovich-like amounts about like small change that could clearly be another option.

Larsson likes the sun but he also likes his football, so the standard of the game in Qatar at the moment may have that destination slipping down the rankings. The smart money is on Spain as Larsson has dropped big hints that the climate and the level of football there may be the ideal scenario for him, Magdalena and their young family as he winds down his career. The world is his oyster but when Larsson's career world has been Hogaborg, Helsinborgs, Feyenoord and Celtic, then the Bhoys must be seen as the pearl in that oyster. A pearl formed by the piece of grit that was Feyenoord and diving for pearls is a risky business. The pressure is great, no pun intended, and there are numerous sharks ready and waiting to snap off a piece of the meat for themselves. So will Larsson settle for the shining pearl of Celtic Football Club and the fans that adore him so much? Will he take missing all that into account as he makes his decision, if he has not already made it? Another Celtic legend is no doubt that Larsson will miss Celtic when he does leave. That legend is none other than the great Jimmy Johnstone.

Jinky was Celtic's original No.7 and in the days before Henrik Larsson masks (dreadlocked or otherwise), nodding dolls, posters, mugs, mouse mats, ceramic plates, CDs, DVDs, bedspreads, towels, T-shirts and anything else you care to mention in the marketing revolution (including books), the wee man was the only instantly recognisable product on the market. This, of course, was in the days when football clubs hadn't latched on to the merchandising market in any way whatsoever. So the Jinky stuff was only available 'Doon the Barras' or on the streets on the way up to the game. And just as the dreadlocks and tongue image became synonymous with Henrik Larsson, just a wee touch of colour on the head – any shade from yellow through ginger to carrot orange – was enough to shift Jinky blow-up dolls, miniature key rings and plastic snowstorms by the box load. But also like Larsson, the hero worship adorned on Jinky wasn't purely because of the aesthetic image, it's because they both possess a talent for making the sport of football entertaining, exciting and worth paying the money to watch.

Sometimes just a few seconds of watching Jinky Johnstone was worth the entrance money alone and could it be mere happenstance that they both donned the No.7. Their paths are inextricably linked. So much so that despite Jinky not being a striker, he was Celtic's top scorer in European football with 16 goals until the arrival of Larsson. And the Celtic legend knows that Larsson will hurt when he leaves Celtic. He said: "First of all, it was a bit of a coup for the club to hold on to Henrik when so many other heroes and stars have left down the years. There were obviously quite a few clubs interested in him and, because of the goals he scores, they would have been ready to pay funny money for him. But I suppose Henrik has done alright for himself on the financial side at Celtic. All he had to do was pitch himself right and, of course, the club wanted to keep him. But you just have to look at Celtic Park and say, why would you want to play anywhere else? The stadium is great and the fans are fantastic. The punters have taken Henrik to their hearts so why would he want to go anywhere else? Celtic are in Europe every year as well. Big Jock used to say to us when we were playing some big European team, what are you worried about them for? They aren't in Europe every year – we are. But the one thing I can say is that when you do leave Celtic, it's a sore one and Henrik will find that out when the time comes."

When Johnstone plied his trade with Celtic, his wing play hugging the touchline while turning defender inside out and corkscrewing them into the turf was such that punters in The Jungle had to stand on tip-toes for fear of missing the next magical touch. He pulled the punters in as much as he pulled the opposing defences apart. But in these days of all-seated stadia, Johnstone is in no doubt as to why, when clubs want to put bums on seats, Larsson, in the nicest possible way of course, lifts bums off seats. He said: "The place rises to him because he is all over the place, he chases back and the big difference is that his games aren't just about goals. He gives 100 per cent all over the park and the Celtic punters love that type of player at Parkhead. That is the sort of football they have been brought up to love. It's the Celtic way and they really appreciate a player with Henrik's attitude to the game. They love a trier and getting the head down and trying is a massive part of Henrik's game. The crowds at Celtic Park have been weaned on those type of players."

Johnstone added: "He injected something into the club at exactly the time they needed it the most. Celtic needed someone who had the ability to grab that half-chance and Henrik is amazing at that. He is a playmaker as well, with lovely wee one-twos which are very effective and vitally important in the box. He's a very unselfish, thoughtful and generous player. He won't shoot just for the sake of it. The game is all about putting the ball in the back of the net and if he sees a team-mate in a better position then he has no qualms whatsoever about laying it off. It's better that the ball goes into the back of the net rather than coming back off the woodwork. What's the use in that? And Henrik shows great judgement when he's on the ball and a team-mate has a clearer view of the goal. He is not a glory hunter."

The No.7 is such a revered number at Celtic Park due to the influence of Johnstone and Larsson that one of the club's restaurants has been named in honour of them. The No.7 Restaurant takes pride of place in the Celtic End with a panoramic view of the hollowed turf where both have written their own pages in the Celtic history books. Johnstone wore the shorts and Larsson wears the shirt but Jinky doesn't see the number as having any magical influence and he is not bothered at all about having any wind taken out of his sails.

He said "It's a different ball game now and we just happen to wear the same number for Celtic. I was an entertainer out on the wing in the days when the numbers 8, 9 and 10 were expected to score all the goals. I scored a few goals myself right enough but the number 7 and 11 were expected to be wide men out on the wing. The numbers game is different these days, with Henrik being number 7 and scoring all the goals. Henrik is a striker and I did well with the number 7, so maybe it is a lucky number. There's no confrontation though, I won the Greatest Ever Celt award but I would have been delighted if it was Henrik. He has deserved all the adulation and accolades. It was voted for by Celtic people and I played a wee bit longer than Henrik for the Hoops."

That 'wee bit longer' included the nine-in-a-row years when he, Billy McNeill and Bobby Lennox were the only Celts to play in every season of that magical period. There was also the small matter of the Wee Man lifting the European Cup in 1967 but an oft-asked question is where would Henrik Larsson have fitted into the scheme of things with the Lisbon Lions? Another is how would Celtic have faired without the Swede over the past seven years? Jinky said: "He's a player so there would be no problem. One of us would have to be injured right enough but he definitely has the ability to play with the Lions. As to the question of the Celtic team without Larsson over the past few years?

They're a team of professionals so they would have coped. It wouldn't have been easy but they would have done it. You only have to look at when he was absent with injury, they still coped. I'm glad they didn't have to do it for too long without him, though. But Henrik came back and well done to him for it. He persevered admirably and when he came back it was as if it never happened. There was that wee bit missing but they coped."

Larsson, of course, is only one member of the team - the Magnificent Eleven as opposed to the Magnificent Seven, and Alan Thompson has played a magnificent part in setting up many of the Larsson goals as well as being on the receiving end of a few Larsson tee-ups himself. Thommo said: "I knew quite a lot about him before I came to Celtic. Obviously that was through the World Cups, European Championships, and playing for Sweden. But ironically not as a Celtic player, not a lot, it was mainly through his games for Sweden. He really measured up to what I had heard about him, though. He's everything that you want in a striker. For someone like myself he's ideal with his running off the ball, it makes my job a lot easier. He definitely makes a lot of jobs a lot easier. He's just an unbelievable individual but if you ask everyone else in the squad you would get the same answer. In his work rate for the team as well as his skills and ability he's second to none.

"And as for the usual talk of him not being able to produce that down in England, I don't have to even go there. Henrik doesn't have to go shouting his mouth off and he doesn't need anyone else to do it for him His record speaks for itself against top class international defenders in top class competitions. His goals are so valuable to us but what sets him apart is that he's someone that can score goals when there's not really a chance there. He's different class really. He's one of these people who create chances for themselves and score when they've no right to. Away from the pitch he's fairly independent really. He keeps himself to himself and is very single-minded - very positive."

Thompson, like many Celts who have arrived from down south, may not have known too much about Larsson but Irishman Neil Lennon comes from a family steeped in the Celtic background and there wasn't much he didn't know about the Swede – that is until he started playing alongside him. Lennon said: "Well, I knew he was a good player, a great goalscorer but obviously I didn't realise just what a player he was. I'm into my fourth season now and he just seems to get better and better.

There seems to be no holding him back. Exactly what he gives to the team is difficult to quantify because he delivers so much. His goals speak for themselves but even they arrive in great variety. There are the headers that he shouldn't have a hope of reaching. There is his almost telepathic reaction in the six-yard box. He can go round keepers with ease when they are expecting a chip and he can chip them when they are waiting for him to go round them. Then there are his free kicks, which are a sight to behold. But it's not just his goals.

"He can make them as well and he is an expert at laying goals off for other players. And his tracking back is a godsend to the midfield and defence at times. He absolutely hates losing the ball and he will give everything in winning it back. He's the ultimate team player. Celtic will definitely miss him when he goes, whether that's at the end of this season or a year or two down the line. The players will miss him on the park but it goes without saying that the support will miss him greatly. He's such a hero to them and he deserves all the adulation. Especially after coming back from injury the way he did."

Should I Stay Or Should I Go, Combat Rock (Side I, Track 3)
"So you gotta let us know"

Back to The Clash again, although the lyric is paraphrased but unfortunately as the song goes, Larsson won't "be here until the end of time." So what will happen? One thing is evident and it is that the players and supporters will miss the talismanic Swede when the end of his time comes, whether that is at the end of the season or further down the line. He may string along with the pearl he found in Celtic but the world is still his lobster, as Del Boy Trotter would say, and it's a big, big world out there despite what we as Celtic fans may think. But if Henrik's departure is imminent, it will mark a new development in the long and not so illustrious chapter of heroes leaving Celtic.

As stated before, there have been mixed feeling when Celtic heroes have departed the environs of Paradise for elsewhere. There were those whose careers were all but finished and they left with the good wishes of all. Then there are those who left at the heights of their careers and some of those left a bad taste in the mouth. And now, if Henrik leaves, despite him still being at the height of his unique powers as far as we Celtic fans are concerned, he will leave with the universal and unanimous good wishes of all concerned with the club. He began season 2003/04 as usual by banging in the goals as well as making them for others, Martin O'Neill was particularly delighted at his two vital and wonderful assists against Lyon in the Champions League group stages. And Celtic supporters throughout the world would give their eye-teeth if Larsson were to score his traditional goal in the first competitive games of the term when season 2004/05. How good would that be?

Larsson here in season 2004/05? That remains in the lap of the gods though, or rather in the lap of Ghod. Larsson is his own man and he plays his cards close to his chest. Would the chance of another Seville-like affair tempt him to stay? But Celtic have been blessed to have had Henrik Larsson at Paradise. In general, punters and pundits are loathe to compare the flavour of the month with the all-time legends of yesteryear – like the fairly recent CD that makes it into the all-time top 10 albums and then a couple of years down the line is nowhere to be seen. But you can put your mortgage on people still writing about Henrik Larsson in 50 and 100 years time. That is a stick on. He is bang in the centre of that portrait of the Celtic greats and there is no way on earth ANYBODY is going to edge him out.

We can only be thankful that Larsson came to Celtic as we have been enriched by his presence. We would love Celtic to be his final club but only if that means him staying here until he's about 36-years-old. And we don't know what the bookies' odds on that are. The current batch of youngsters coming along to support Celtic have never known a hero like him – and that goes for some of the not so young ones as well. But Larsson giving up the game completely just now would be akin to someone stealing the Mona Lisa from The Louvre and keeping it in a dungeon somewhere. Talent like Larsson's should not be lost to the world and please don't let it be lost to Celtic. We are greedy here and we make no bones about it.

We are the same greedy fans who wanted the UEFA Cup AND the championship. But we ended up with nothing. We can live that life. We have lived with nothing before but we have always strived against it and it's good to know that the club are going to strive to keep Henrik Larsson. But maybe he has already made his mind up. As The Clash song goes "always tease, tease, tease". But one of the reasons we love

Larsson is his ability to tease defences in Scotland and at the very top of the tree in Europe.

In the opening chapter of this tribute to the great Henrik Larsson, the Dutch influence, on both sides of the coin, was paramount in the Swede coming to Paradise and the acorn from which the mighty Dutch oak grew was Faas Wilkes. But when Wilkes was asked on his retirement if he was going into coaching, he answered: "Football was my profession, not my life." Despite Larsson's wonderful ability with a ball at his feet, that may well be Larsson's philosophy on life also – and that may make his decision for him.

Thanks Henrik, you really made us happy when skies were really grey.

Statistics

Date of Birth: 20/09/71   Place of Birth: Helsinborg, Sweden
Height: 5'9"   Weight: 11st 2lbs
Former clubs: Hogaborg, Helsinborgs, Feyenoord   Debut: Hibernian v Celtic, 03/08/97
International Caps: 72   International goals: 24

The Larsson Lottery
Henrik Larsson's Celtic goals up until the end of season 2002/03

#	Date	Comp	Opponent	#	Date	Comp	Opponent
1	Aug 9, 97	LC	Berwick Rangers.	51	Mar 8, 99	SC	Morton
2	Aug 23, 97	SPL	St Johnstone	52	Mar 14, 99	SPL	Aberdeen
3	Sep 10, 97	LC	Motherwell	53	Mar 14, 99	SPL	Aberdeen
4	Sep 20, 97	SPL	Aberdeen	54	Apr 3, 99	SPL	Dundee
5	Sep 20, 97	SPL	Aberdeen	55	Apr 3, 99	SPL	Dundee
6	Oct 4, 97	SPL	Kilmarnock	56	Apr 17, 99	SPL	Motherwell
7	Oct 4, 97	SPL	Kilmarnock	57	Aug 1, 99	SPL	Aberdeen
8	Oct 18, 97	SPL	Hearts	58	Aug 1, 99	SPL	Aberdeen
9	Oct 25, 97	SPL	St Johnstone	59	Aug 12, 99	EURO	Cwmbran Town
10	Nov 1, 97	SPL	Dunfermline	60	Aug 12, 99	EURO	Cwmbran Town
11	Nov 22, 97	SPL	Dundee Utd	61	Aug 21, 99	SPL	Dundee
12	Nov 22, 97	SPL	Dundee Utd	62	Aug 29, 99	SPL	Hearts
13	Nov 30, 97	LC	Dundee Utd	63	Sep 16, 99	EURO	Tel Aviv
14	Dec 9, 97	SPL	Aberdeen	64	Sep 16, 99	EURO	Tel Aviv
15	Dec 20, 97	SPL	Hibernian	65	Sep 30, 99	EURO	Tel Aviv
16	Feb 2, 98	SPL	Aberdeen	66	Oct 16, 99	SPL	Aberdeen
17	Feb 25, 98	SPL	Dunfermline	67	Oct 16, 99	SPL	Aberdeen
18	Apr 8, 98	SPL	Kilmarnock	68	Oct 16, 99	SPL	Aberdeen
19	May 9, 98	SPL	St Johnstone	69	Jul 30, 00	SPL	Dundee Utd
20	Jul 29, 98	Euro	St Patrick's Athletic	70	Aug 10, 00	EURO	Jeunesse Esch
21	Aug 16, 98	SPL	Aberdeen	71	Aug 13, 00	SPL	Kilmarnock
22	Aug 16, 98	SPL	Aberdeen	72	Aug 19, 00	SPL	Hearts
23	Sep 15, 98	Euro	Vitoria Guimaraes	73	Aug 27, 00	SPL	Rangers.
24	Sep 29, 98	Euro	Vitoria Guimaraes	74	Aug 27, 00	SPL	Rangers.
25	Oct 17, 98	SPL	Dunfermline	75	Sep 09, 00	SPL	Hibernian
26	Nov 3, 98	Euro	Zurich	76	Sep 09, 00	SPL	Hibernian
27	Nov 7, 98	SPL	Dundee	77	Sep 14, 00	EURO	HJK Helsinki
28	Nov 7, 98	SPL	Dundee	78	Sep 14, 00	EURO	HJK Helsinki
29	Nov 7, 98	SPL	Dundee	79	Sep 17, 00	SPL	Dunfermline
30	Nov 14, 98	SPL	St Johnstone	80	Sep 17, 00	SPL	Dunfermline
31	Nov 21, 98	SPL	Rangers.	81	Oct 1, 00	SPL	Aberdeen
32	Nov 21, 98	SPL	Rangers.	82	Oct 14, 00	SPL	St Mirren
33	Nov 28, 98	SPL	Motherwell	83	Oct 17, 00	SPL	St Johnstone
34	Dec 12, 98	SPL	Dundee Utd	84	Oct 21, 00	SPL	Dundee Utd
35	Dec 19, 98	SPL	Dunfermline	85	Oct 26, 00	EURO	Bordeaux
36	Dec 19, 98	SPL	Dunfermline	86	Nov 12, 00	SPL	St Johnstone
37	Jan 3, 99	SPL	Rangers.	87	Nov 12, 00	SPL	St Johnstone
38	Jan 23, 99	SC	Airdrie	88	Nov 18, 00	SPL	Hearts
39	Jan 31, 99	SPL	St Johnstone	89	Nov 18, 00	SPL	Hearts
40	Feb 6, 99	SPL	Hearts	90	Nov 26, 00	SPL	Rangers.
41	Feb 6, 99	SPL	Hearts	91	Dec 2, 00	SPL	Dunfermline
42	Feb 6, 99	SPL	Hearts	92	Dec 15, 00	SPL	Aberdeen
43	Feb 13, 99	SC	Dunfermline	93	Dec 15, 00	SPL	Aberdeen
44	Feb 13, 99	SC	Dunfermline	94	Dec 15, 00	SPL	Aberdeen
45	Feb 13, 99	SC	Dunfermline	95	Dec 23, 00	SPL	St Mirren
46	Feb 21, 99	SPL	Motherwell	96	Dec 26, 00	SPL	Dundee Utd
47	Feb 21, 99	SPL	Motherwell	97	Jan 02, 01	SPL	Kilmarnock
48	Feb 21, 99	SPL	Motherwell	98	Jan 02, 01	SPL	Kilmarnock
49	Feb 21, 99	PL	Motherwell	99	Jan 02, 01	SPL	Kilmarnock
50	Feb 27, 99	SPL	Dundee Utd	100	Jan 02, 01	SPL	Kilmarnock

101	Feb 04, 01	SPL	Hearts	165	Sep 19, 02	EURO	FK Suduva
102	Feb 04, 01	SPL	Hearts	166	Sep 22, 02	SPL	Dundee
103	Feb 04, 01	SPL	Hearts	167	Sep 28, 02	SPL	Kilmarnock
104	Feb 07, 01	LC	Rangers.	168	Sep 28, 02	SPL	Kilmarnock
105	Feb 07, 01	LC	Rangers.	169	Sep 28, 02	SPL	Kilmarnock
106	Feb 17, 01	SC	Dunfermline	170	Oct 6, 02	SPL	Rangers.
107	Feb 17, 01	SC	Dunfermline	171	Oct 6, 02	SPL	Rangers.
108	Mar 4, 01	SPL	Dunfermline	172	Oct 20, 02	SPL	Hearts
109	Mar 07, 01	SC	Dunfermline	173	Oct 20, 02	SPL	Hearts
110	Mar 07, 01	SC	Dunfermline	174	Oct 27, 02	SPL	Dunfermline
111	Mar 11, 01	SC	Hearts	175	Oct 31, 02	EURO	Blackburn Rovers
112	Mar 14, 01	SPL	St Johnstone	176	Nov 3, 02	SPL	Aberdeen
113	Mar 18, 01	LC	Kilmarnock	177	Nov 14, 02	EURO	Blackburn Rovers
114	Mar 18, 01	LC	Kilmarnock	178	Nov 17, 02	SPL	Partick Thistle
115	Mar 18, 01	LC	Kilmarnock	179	Nov 24, 02	SPL	Livingston
116	Apr 15, 01	SC	Dundee Utd	180	Nov 24, 02	SPL	Livingston
117	Apr 15, 01	SC	Dundee Utd	181	Nov 28, 02	EURO	Celta Vigo
118	Apr 29, 01	SPL	Rangers.	182	Dec 1, 02	SPL	Motherwell
119	May 6, 01	SPL	Hibernian	183	Dec 21, 02	SPL	Dundee
120	May 26, 01	SC	Hibernian	184	Dec 26, 02	SPL	Hearts
121	May 26, 01	SC	Hibernian	185	Dec 29, 02	SPL	Dunfermline
122	Aug 4, 01	SPL	Kilmarnock	186	Jan 2, 03	SPL	Aberdeen
123	Aug 11, 01	SPL	Hearts	187	Jan 25, 03	SC	St Mirren
124	Aug 11, 01	SPL	Hearts	188	Jan 25, 03	SC	St Mirren
125	Aug 25, 01	SPL	Hibernian	189	Jan 29, 03	SPL	Dundee Utd
126	Sep 15, 01	SPL	Dundee	190	Feb 6, 03	LC	Dundee Utd
127	Sep 15, 01	SPL	Dundee	191	Mar 13, 03	EURO	Liverpool
128	Sep 18, 01	EURO	Juventus	192	Mar 16, 03	LC	Rangers.
129	Sep 22, 01	SPL	Aberdeen	193	Apr 10, 03	EURO	Boavista
130	Sep 25, 01	EURO	Porto	194	Apr 13, 03	SPL	Kilmarnock
131	Oct 13, 01	SPL	Motherwell	195	Apr 19, 03	SPL	Hearts
132	Oct 31, 01	EURO	Juventus	196	Apr 24, 03	EURO	Boavista
133	Nov 3, 01	SPL	St Johnstone	197	May 3, 03	SPL	Dunfermline
134	Nov 17, 01	SPL	Hearts	198	May 14, 03	SPL	Dundee
135	Nov 25, 01	SPL	Rangers.	199	May 21, 03	EURO	Porto
136	Dec 6, 01	EURO	Valencia	200	May 21, 03	EURO	Porto
137	Dec 15, 01	SPL	Dundee				
138	Dec 26, 01	SPL	Livingston				
139	Dec 26, 01	SPL	Livingston				
140	Dec 29, 01	SPL	Dundee Utd				
141	Jan 2, 02	SPL	Motherwell				
142	Jan 19, 02	SPL	St Johnstone				
143	Jan 23, 02	SPL	Hearts				
144	Jan 23, 02	SPL	Hearts				
145	Jan 26, 02	SC	Kilmarnock				
146	Jan 30, 02	SPL	Livingston				
147	Feb 8, 02	SPL	Dunfermline				
148	Feb 8, 02	SPL	Dunfermline				
149	Feb 8, 02	SPL	Dunfermline				
150	Feb 17, 02	SPL	Dundee				
151	Mar 19, 02	SPL	Motherwell				
152	Mar 19, 02	SPL	Motherwell				
153	Mar 23, 02	SC	Ayr Utd				
154	Apr 6, 02	SPL	Livingston				
155	Apr 6, 02	SPL	Livingston				
156	Apr 6, 02	SPL	Livingston				
157	Aug 3, 02	SPL	Dunfermline				
158	Aug 3, 02	SPL	Dunfermline				
159	Aug 14, 02	EURO	FC Basel				
160	Aug 17, 02	SPL	Dundee Utd				
161	Aug 24, 02	SPL	Partick Thistle				
162	Sep 1, 02	SPL	Livingston				
163	Sep 19, 02	EURO	FK Suduva				
164	Sep 19, 02	EURO	FK Suduva				

The breakdown season by season

Season	L	LC	SC	Euro	Total
1997/98	16	3	-	-	19
1998/99	28	-	5	4	37
1999/00	7	-	-	5	12
2000/01	35	5	9	4	53
2001/02	29	-	2	4	35
2002/03	28	2	2	12	44
Total	143	10	18	29	200

Who the goals were scored against

Dunfermline	24	Cwmbran Town	2
Hearts	21	HJK Helsinki	2
Aberdeen	20	Juventus	2
Kilmarnock	17	Partick Thistle	2
Dundee United	14	Vitoria Guimaraes	2
Dundee	13	Berwick Rangers	1
Rangers	13	St Patrick's Athletic	1
Motherwell	12	FC Zurich	1
St Johnstone	11	Airdrie	1
Livingston	9	Morton	1
Hibernian	7	Jeunesse Esch	1
St Mirren	4	Bordeaux	1
FK Suduva	3	Valencia	1
Hapoel Tel Aviv	3	Ayr United	1
Porto	3	Basel	1
Blackburn Rovers	2	Celta Vigo	1
Boavista	2	Liverpool	1